CAD for Fashion Design

Renée Weiss Chase

College of Design Arts,
Drexel University

Prentice Hall
Upper Saddle River, NJ 07458

Library of Congress Cataloging-in-Publication Data

Chase, Renée Weiss
    CAD for fashion design / Renée Weiss Chase.
      p. cm.
    Includes bibliographical references and index.
    ISBN 0-13-373242-8
    1. Costume design—Data processing.   2. Computer-aided design.
  I. Title.
TT507.C5238   1997
687'.0285—dc20
                                                          96-1694
                                                              CIP

Acquisitions Editor: Elizabeth Sugg
Director of Production and Manufacturing: Bruce Johnson
Managing Editor: Mary Carnis
Editorial/Production Supervision and
   Interior Design: Tally Morgan, WordCrafters Editorial Services, Inc.
Cover Design: Kenji Takabayashi, ComputerDesign, Inc.
Manufacturing Buyer: Edward O'Dougherty
Marketing Manager: Danny Hoyt

 © 1997 by Prentice-Hall, Inc.
A Division of Simon & Schuster / a Viacom Company
Upper Saddle River, New Jersey 07458

Printed in the United States of America

10 9 8 7 6 5 4 3 2 1

ISBN 0-13-373242-8

PRENTICE HALL INTERNATIONAL (UK) LIMITED, *London*
PRENTICE HALL OF AUSTRALIA PTY. LIMITED, *Sydney*
PRENTICE HALL CANADA INC., *Toronto*
PRENTICE HALL HISPANOAMERICANA, S.A., *Mexico*
PRENTICE HALL OF INDIA PRIVATE LIMITED, *New Delhi*
PRENTICE HALL OF JAPAN, INC., *Tokyo*
PRENTICE HALL OF SOUTHEAST ASIA PTE. LTD., *Singapore*
EDITORIA PRENTICE HALL DO BRASIL, LTDA., *Rio de Janeiro*

This book is dedicated to
Charlotte Weiss
who shines her light eternally
on my path

and to my collective heart
Fred, Danielle, and Jesse

Table of Contents

Foreword

In the slow Dark Ages ("B.C.A.D."), few could fathom the depth of change that would occur. While it was thrilling to project the possibilities, reality has surpassed all expectations. I have always been an idea person without the skill to render. The C.A.D. gives me the ability to realize what I visualize, to test and correct and eventually soar.

Image your imagination! This is technicolour dreaming that doesn't go away, that you can control. Ladies and gentlemen, start your engines!! The race has started and it's your turn to drive. . . . . Warp speed. . . . . Weft speed. . . . . Idea speed. . . . .

Alexander Julian

Preface

Technology has paved the way for the ever-changing, highly accelerated fashion world to offer product more quickly, less expensively, and in greater abundance than ever before. Consumers have demanded it, retailers have prodded manufacturers, and technology has offered the means by which every fashion supplier's goal—better product at a better price—can be realized.

In two short decades, we have reached a point at which many preproduction processes are simplified, if not eliminated, and at which digital printing is on the verge of redefining the world's textile industry. The idea of interconnectivity, which links information from computer to computer all over the world, is becoming a reality both in terms of the design and manufacture of the product and in terms of merchandising and marketing that product.

The application of the new technology began with the modification of production processes. Now technology is impacting design processes, and product development cycles are being shortened dramatically. Electronic data information systems (EDI) have made tracking and stocking of merchandise at the retail level exponentially easier than they were ten years ago. Exact records of a particular customer's buying patterns can be analyzed to provide personalized marketing strategies that lead to enhanced sales.

At the consumer level, customers have the option of doing their shopping right from their homes at computer workstations. They can view fashion shows or catalogues or even retail store interiors on their CD-ROM drives. They can place an order by FAX or E-Mail. If they prefer a traditional retail environment, they can go to certain stores and be measured by video camera for a pair of custom-made jeans. Or they can feel secure in purchasing a new sofa because a computer has already shown what the fabric swatch will look like draped over the frame and stuffing of the sofa they selected.

The technologies briefly mentioned here have brought about enormous changes in the textile and apparel industries. Refinements and extensions of the technologies are constantly happening at all levels of design and production. Employees of the textile and apparel industries are partners in the evolution of the technologies and will benefit from and be stimulated by the exciting advancements in their professions.

This book is an attempt to offer a picture of some of the technological changes that have emerged in the fashion world and to provide students with a way of integrating this technology with the process of designing clothes. It is also an attempt to provide this information in a nontechnical way.

Systems that are in actual use in industry will be described and if a college or university has the advantage of owning one of these systems and training their design and fashion merchandising students to use it, all the better. For those schools, this book may serve as a reference and possibly as a way to organize a curriculum on the topic of CAD. For programs that do not have industry-specific systems, this book will provide ways of simulating industrial CAD output using commercial, off-the-shelf graphics programs.

This book focuses on the representational and graphic aspects of fashion design. Textile design is discussed primarily in terms of visualization rather than in terms of the technical requirements of printing, weaving, and knitting. Information on production processes such as patternmaking, grading, and markermaking will be offered descriptively rather than technically.

This book is organized into eight chapters. The first is the history of computer-aided design followed by a description of the types of systems presently utilized in the industry and the role each plays in the design process. Chapter 1 presents an overview with a broad-based perspective rather than an abundance of technical information. The remaining chapters break down the design process and describe the CAD-related experiences that a designer might encounter while on the job. Exercises that simulate industry practices in each phase of design are offered and the accompanying disk provides files and images for the execution of the problems. (Approximately 5MB of available memory is required to use the disk.) The problems build on each other so that in the final chapter, Presentation and Graphics, the student will be able to produce a finished product.

Interviews with CAD designers and personal photographs of these designers in their work environments are an important part of each chapter. They provide a student with exposure to real-world experiences and job descriptions that an academic text can only allude to.

We assume that the student has some mastery of basic computer functions and a familiarity with one of the suggested software programs offered in the introduction. If this is not the case, then basic tutorials for the graphics software should be undertaken prior to using this book.

Acknowledgments

Thanks to my professional associates and all those in the CAD industry who generously answered questions, offered demonstrations, and lent support for this project. Thanks also to all of my students past and present who continually challenge, inspire, and reward my efforts.

Special appreciation to:

Laura Satori: Photography
Christina Kuo: Software research, flat sketches
Kathi Martin Maddaloni: Textile designs
Lauren Sphar: Textile designs
Roberta Hochberger Gruber: Fashion illustrations
Kenji Takabayashi: Cover design
Lee Albright: Graphics
Jamie Durkin: Acquisitions and permissions
Jan Marshall: Presentation boards
Peter Bartscherer: Technical support
Alison Grudier: Technical consultation

Walter Wilhelm, Gerber Garment Technologies; David Matsil, Monarch Computex; Maureen Behl, Jones Apparel Group; Lori Catlin Garcia, Kathryn Chamberlin, and Jay Constantino, Women's Specialty Retailing Group; Jennifer Provest, Alps Sportswear Manufacturing Co., Inc.; Jane Pigush and Kay Fritz, Land's End Corporation; Janet Hamlin and Julie Kanberg, GAP.

Michael Adams, Carol Fisher, Deborah Sheesley, Kari Souders, Qun Wang, Blair Levin, David Raizman, Ivy Strickler, Chanda Butler.

Phontella Ruff, Dolores Quinn, Phyllis Feldkamp, Miriam Kessler, Ruth Simon, Fred Chase, Florence Mehr, Judie Mangel.

About the Author

Renée Weiss Chase is a tenured professor at Drexel University. She is also Head of Fashion Design with programs at both the undergraduate and graduate levels and teaches upper level fashion studio courses.

Chase first introduced Computer Aided Design for fashion at Drexel in 1986. Her initial research was supported through a series of grants. One result was the development of two "CAD in Fashion" courses which have been running at peak capacity since 1990. Graduates of Chase's classes have become professional CAD designers in fashion and textile design.

Chase has a Bachelor of Science Degree in Fashion Design and a Master's Degree in Science and Technical Communcation. She spent ten years in industry as a sportswear designer and manufacturer. She also spent two years as a fashion journalist.

Her first book, *Design Without Limits,* focuses on designing clothes for the physically challenged.

Chapter 1

Introduction

Picture this scenario: You are part of a design team working on a new collection. You sit at a computer and shop for the fabrics for your line. Descriptions and visual samples are available to you on line. You can modify the fabric, recolor it—the possibilities are limitless. Then you can try the fabric out as a garment.

You call your model onto the screen and drape the fabric over the image of her body. If you are working on last season's suit, you can update the silhouette and change details, modify proportions or go back to the beginning and alter the fabric again. You're not sure your customer will like the result, so you call up the buyer wherever in the world he or she may be and he or she joins you on line. Together you make adjustments to the garment.

On to production. Everything you have decided about that garment—all the specifications—accompany your image as it goes to the patternmaking area, the markermaking and cutting areas, and even to sales and marketing. Each person who works on your garment at each stage of design, production, and sales adds technical information to the file and that file is accessible to any selected person in the chain.

Once you have designed your product line, you have complete control over the way it is presented in the stores. You can instruct your computer to fold your shirts and arrange them on a display stand by color right next to the pants and shorts they coordinate with. These specifications are also added to the file so that every store that carries your line arranges your display in the same way.

At the point of sale—the retail store—sales data are entered so your company will know how quickly the style is selling and in what colors, and when a reorder shipment will be required. This information is relayed to your company instantly. If your company is interested in direct mail or in-store marketing, you can create a whole multimedia event on CD ROM with supermodels walking down a catwalk wearing the clothes you designed. It doesn't matter that in all probability not a single sample has been made!

This scenario paints an exciting picture. As you might expect, it isn't as simple as it seems. Every person in the chain—from designer to production manager to patternmaker and sales manager—must be a well-trained technician who knows how to instruct computers to do the work. But it is a much different scene than that of the past in which bringing a product to market and tracking that product involved a pencil instead of a mouse or stylus, and an adding machine instead of a spreadsheet program.

WHAT IS CAD?

CAD is computer-aided design. Any part of the design process that can utilize the computer as a tool fits under the CAD umbrella. Originally, the term CAD was used in various industries to refer primarily to functions that required drafting of precision machine parts and working with highly technical specifications. In the textile and apparel industries, CAD has come to include graphics applications used for purposes of visualizing design as well as technical specifications and functions.

Some systems which will be described later in this book are used for the manufacturing end of textiles and apparel as well as the design segment. These are referred to as CAD/CAM systems (computer-aided design/computer-aided manufacture). The divisions between the two have become more and more nebulous and the term CIM (computer-integrated manufacture) appeared as a way to synthesize these two directions. For purposes of this book, the more popular term, CAD, will be used to describe both the design and manufacturing segments.

CAD was originally developed on industry-specific or **turnkey** systems. This means that the manufacturers of CAD equipment created their own proprietary hardware and software and sold the entire package to the apparel industry. These turnkey systems are used widely, but have also been prohibitively expensive for a small manufacturer. As a result, industrious employees and entrepreneurs began simulating the properties and the potential of the turnkey systems with off-the-shelf or commercially available software. As a matter of fact, many companies that do own turnkey systems supplement them with commercial software packages.

In a survey polling CAD users in the apparel industry, reports indicated that among PC users, 17 percent use commercial art/illustration programs, 12 percent use desktop publishing programs, and 2 percent use multimedia programs. Among Macintosh users, 36 percent use art/illustration programs, 9 percent use desktop publishing programs, and 9 percent use multimedia programs.[1]

It is a given that CAD is a mainstream tool; companies that hope to compete in the fashion marketplace, especially at the mass level, cannot prosper without some level of CAD technology. At this point, most companies have integrated some form of CAD technology into their design and production processes. An estimated 20,000 CAD systems are in place worldwide.[2] Much of this technology lies in the realm of patternmaking and markermaking, much in the arena of textile design and production. But the strongest trend is toward complete computer integration from design and product development through to merchandising and business operations on a worldwide network.

The National Knitwear Association and A. Grudier Consulting conducted a survey of 228 apparel manufacturers which indicated that:

65% use CAD to create colorways
60% use CAD to create printed fabric design
48% use CAD to create merchandising presentations
41% use CAD to create knit designs.[3]

The demonstrated benefits of CAD include "increased productivity, reduced product development time, increased creativity to improve conceptual designs, high product design capability, reduced cost of samples and prototypes, and reduced turnaround time."[4] Designers can explore a myriad of visual possibilities without the cost of making samples or strike-offs. Computer capacities offer immediate response and gratification. Finally, CAD has the potential to create seamless and universally understood communications among all phases of operation, a capacity that can save manufacturers a great deal of time and money.

The role of computers in the textile and apparel industries no doubt will continue to grow. In order to be prepared for the work force in the fashion industries, students must have some familiarity, if not competency, with the computer as a tool. Ultimately, the industry is looking for designers and merchandisers who are not necessarily familiar with one particular system, but who are computer literate and operative and who have as much flexibility and comfort with the computer as a tool as they do with conventional, hand-executed methods.

It is important, though, that we keep in mind that the goal in this learning process is to take advantage of the creative possibilities that a computer can offer a designer or merchandiser. One of the great advantages to the designer in using a computer is that so many more ideas can be expressed than the designer would have time to accomplish by hand. A range of pocket styles can be tried on a basic jacket silhouette in a moment; the collar size and shape can be varied just as quickly. A fabric painting can take a full day to do by hand, whereas a dozen recolorings can be done in a day with the aid of a computer. All of this means that design choices and possibilities can be infinite *if the designer is given the time and freedom to be creative and to experiment using the systems*. Most of the time, the designer has a specific job to do: a print to recolor or a stripe to create as a complement to the print that is preestablished by the customer or the merchandiser. A pressing deadline is always at hand, and as a result, many design possibilities using CAD remain unexplored.

We are not trying to produce CAD operators whose role is to "run the machine" for the designer. Unfortunately, this is the case in some companies and opportunities to explore the creative potential of the computer are not offered to the employees who use the systems. Their roles in these situations are to provide services to the design team. While this may be a good situation for some designers, it may be too limited for others. It is very important in any job interview to understand the parameters of the potential job.

Learning how to use a computer for design or patternmaking does not preclude acquiring all of the basic skills of a designer. Over and over we have heard the phrase, "the computer is just another tool." Computers simply aid in the process; they serve as tools for designers, patternmakers, and so on, but they cannot replace the skills required to generate a first pattern, or the experience it takes to check a nest of graded patterns for accuracy. Computers will never be assumed to have the color sense or the eye for proportion and detail that a designer feels intuitively. They will never be able to weed out the good designs from the bad ones. CAD is a tool, like a paintbrush, pencil, hip curve, or calculator. When combined with finely honed skills and sensibilities, the computer helps professionals in the apparel industry achieve beautiful, saleable clothing. The benefits are numerous—speed, accuracy, productivity, communication—but only humans possess the most important tool of the trade—imagination.

BEFORE USING THIS BOOK

You may use any computer platform and operating system along with this book. A Macintosh, PC, or any clone with a Macintosh or Windows operating system is fine. Many graphics programs can be used to complete the exercises in this book, but a few that have been tested include:

For Macintosh	*For PC's*
ClarisWorks®	Deneba Canvas™
Deneba Canvas™	Intelidraw
Adobe Illustrator®	Fractal Design Painter
Freehand™	Corel Draw™
Adobe Photoshop™	Adobe Illustrator®
Fractal Design Painter	Adobe Photoshop™

These recommended choices range in price from about $100 to $700. Of course, each program will have its own particular functions, but in most cases, for representational purposes, a student will be able to achieve the results expected in this book with most paint programs or a combination of drawing and paint pro-

Figure 1–1   The *a* on the left was created in a raster-based paint program; the *a* on the right was created in a vector-based drawing program.

grams. Again, the goal here is to simulate industry practices, not to produce textile designs that are technically ready for engraving and weaving, or artwork that is camera-ready for catalogue development. It is a means of experiencing the process using a computer rather than more traditional drawing and coloring methods.

There are advantages to using a drawing program in certain instances and then importing the drawing into a paint program for coloring. Since drawing programs are **vector based**, line drawings of garments and motifs will be easier to accomplish and the lines will print smoothly at any resolution. The size of the files will also be smaller.

Raster-based displays, also called **bitmapped images,** are offered by paint programs. The tools create a product that is a series of pixels rather than line. More colors are available in raster-based programs and scanning is easier to accomplish. Figure 1–1 shows a comparison between output of text created with a vector-based and a raster-based program. Experiment with both a drawing program and a paint program to experience the differences.

When selecting a graphics program to use for apparel and textile design, the most desirable functions to look for include: (1) the ability to create a custom brush or paint with a custom pattern; and (2) the ability to define, modify, and save a custom palette. Even if your software does not have these capabilities, you will still be able to do the problems using other methods. It is expected, however, that you are completely familiar with your software *before* you use this book. Be certain that you check the memory requirements of the software that you intend to use for compatibility with your system.

HARDWARE

The larger the screen size of your monitor, the better. With a large screen you are able to see a large number of pixels. The most common display monitors show 640 × 480 pixels or 1024 × 756 pixels. The greater the screen resolution—dpi (dots per inch) or dot pitch—the clearer the image. The standard resolution is 72 dpi, but many high-end monitors offer much higher resolutions.

The other factor that affects the image is the type of graphics board installed in your computer. Graphics boards support various numbers of bits per pixel. A bit is the smallest amount of binary information used by the computer and graphics boards operate on an 8-, 12-, 16- or 32-bit-per-pixel system. The greater the **bit depth** the greater the number of colors that can be displayed. An 8-bit graphics board is standard. It will display 256 colors. A 16-bit board is also very common; it will display 32,768 colors. A 24-bit board displays 16.7 million!

Of course, a keyboard and a mouse are necessary components of a workstation. Access to a tablet and a stylus for input is also highly recommended. Drawing with a stylus is similar to working with a pen or pencil; many are pressure-sensitive and offer a good simulation of traditional drawing and painting methods.

Another important input devise is a scanner. They are available in black and white, greyscale, and color. One of the advantages of using a flatbed scanner lies in being able to transfer existing artwork, other images, or found objects into the computer. Once you have scanned them in you are free to alter and manipulate them in myriad ways. Scanning in an image usually requires a good deal of memory space on the hard disk. The higher the resolution of the scan, the more memory is required. This can become problematic if you need to copy your work to a floppy disk which has limited space. If you use a relatively low resolution scan (72 dpi) and you also work at a screen resolution of 72 dpi, you will reduce memory problems as well as problems with scale in the final printout. Scanning techniques will be discussed in greater detail in Chapter 8.

A CD-ROM drive is a valuable, but not absolutely necessary, asset when selecting hardware. As the cost of technology decreases, it may become viable to buy a CD-ROM writer which will enable a large amount of information to be stored on a small disk and eliminate the need for traditional floppies. A number of swatch libraries is commercially available on CD-ROM along with clip art, textures, and so forth that can be incorporated into your design work.

PRINTERS

If you are interested in looking at a hard copy of your work, a printer is important. A variety of printers are available including inkjet, thermal jet, laser, and dye sublimation. The high-end printers, Iris and Stork®, are extremely expensive, but produce images on paper or fabric that are superbly realistic. Most CAD users use laser printers; homes and schools often can only afford inkjet printers. Matching color from your screen to the printed output is a challenge that will be discussed in Chapter 8.

Please note that many art supply stores and printing stores will produce hard copy from a disk at a reasonable price. Service bureaus that offer the highest quality output are also available, but are also much more expensive. So it is not always necessary to own a high-quality output device.

Chapter 2

Computers and the Fashion Industry

HOW IT ALL GOT STARTED

Dallas, Texas, in the early 1970s was the site of the most important revolution in apparel production since the invention of the sewing machine more than 100 years earlier. Ron Martell, who is now referred to as the father of CAD, was actively involved in coming up with a way to use the potential of growing computer technology in the realm of clothing production. This was a very novel idea because patternmaking, sewing, and cutting have always been finely honed crafts that take years to develop. It seemed worthwhile to explore the possibility of using a machine to speed up the production process and increase profits at the same time.

One of the greatest expenditures in clothing production lies in the cost of fabric. Ron Martell and his partner, Don Thayer, set out to reduce the many hours it took for a **markermaker** or **lay planner** to make a marker by hand, and to decrease the amount of fabric used in a garment by producing a marker that fit pattern parts together more economically than an operator could do by hand. The first step in the process was to devise a way for individual pattern shapes to be recorded electronically. From there, the patterns would have to be **graded** (scaled up and down in size) and then all the pattern pieces in each required size would be arranged in the most economical way based on the width parameters of the fabric being used for that particular style. This initial goal led Martell and Thayer to form a company that grew to be a leader in the marketplace, Camsco. One of Camsco's first customers was a little enterprise known as Levi Strauss, which now has CAD systems all over the world.

For Martell and Thayer, the first step in getting a computer to work with a pattern was to define that pattern to the computer. The overall shape of a pattern could be interpreted by the X, Y coordinates of a series of selected points around and within the pattern piece. The operator fed this information into the computer in a process known as **digitizing**. The operator used a small instrument

7

like a magnifying glass with crosshairs at the center to click on the pattern points. The computer translated these to X, Y coordinates on the display terminal. Today, large scanners are used to input pattern shapes and digitizing functions have been minimized.

The next step was to instruct the computer to grade a pattern, which meant to make the pattern piece grow or shrink in a specific way at each of those X, Y coordinates. These instructions are known as **grade rules**. When the pattern shapes were entered in the computer, they would appear in small scale on the markermaker's screen and could then be moved around and finally placed in the best arrangement for maximum fabric utilization. The resulting marker proved to be more efficient than that made by hand and ultimately yielded great savings in material costs for the manufacturer.

During the same period, Burlington Industries and later Genesco, a footwear manufacturer, approached Hughes Aircraft Company in order to develop a single-ply **laser cutter** for use in industry. These cutters went into production in the menswear industry, but no CAD systems existed at this point to drive the cutting machines.

Simultaneously, experts at Hughes, headed by another forerunner in the CAD industry, Walter Wilhelm, combined forces with a menswear company in Baltimore, Wallmuth Tailored Clothing Company, to create a markermaking system. This was called the Autographic System, which later became the AM1 system.

Now, Hughes Aircraft Company had to find a way of printing out their patterns and markers in full scale. They turned to an American manufacturer of cutters and **plotters**, Gerber, a name which has made an indelible imprint on the world of apparel, for help with output. Gerber then built a plotter to be used with the AM1 system and eventually bought the rights to AM1, establishing itself as a direct competitor of Camsco.

In 1978, Ron Martell sold his ownership in Camsco and convinced Walter Wilhelm of Hughes Aircraft to join him in a new venture. And that is how Microdynamics was born. By the end of the 1970s, a Spanish company, Investronica, entered the CAD arena and also directed its efforts at developing a grading and markermaking system. A few years later, Lectra, a firm based in France, joined the scene to establish the fifth CAD company worldwide. Then, Gerber acquired Camsco and the Gerber/Camsco organization came into being. At this time, all CAD systems operated on Hewlett Packard mini computers. The only exception was Microdynamics which used PCs.

During this period in Germany, four computer experts who had worked as European representatives for the American CAD companies recognized a void in the marketplace. Because they had been working directly with apparel manufacturers, they heard about the need for software that could help reduce work time and costs even further than the digitizing systems had thus far. This next step in the evolution of CAD allowed **blocks** or basic patterns (sometimes called **slopers**) to be stored in the computer and all hand functions, such as moving darts, creating pleats, and adding flare, could be accomplished on screen. The result was a **pattern design system (PDS)** that the patternmaker could use to call up basic blocks. He or she could then use the software to manipulate the pattern shapes. In this way, new patterns for new designs could be created on screen from preexisting patterns rather than being drafted by hand and then digitized. These new patterns could then be assigned grade rules and a marker could be made. The digitizing step could then be minimized, if not eliminated. This new German company, Assyst, added further excitement to the field by offering the possibility of interconnectivity—linking a number of computers together in a factory and passing information back and forth among them.

These five pioneers, Gerber/Camsco, Microdynamics, Lectra, Investronica, and Assyst, changed the face of apparel production forever. In 1994, Gerber, which had changed its name to Gerber Garment Technology, merged with Microdynamics and CAD in the United States came full circle. Many, many companies have joined these four in today's CAD marketplace (see Figure 2–1) and have broadened the scope of computer involvement in design, production, and merchandising. One of the technologies that helped to enhance and develop all CAD applications was computer graphics. Companies such as Computer Design Inc., Shima Seiki, Cadtex, ModaCAD™, and others took advantage of advancements in the graphics arena to create design systems for visualization and simulation of fabrics and silhouettes. Visualization systems for all platforms evolved; Monarch Computex used its history in knit production to introduce a visualization program for knits on the Macintosh.

The textile industry had outrun the apparel industry in terms of computer integration far earlier. J. M. Jacquard had patented a loom in 1801 in which punch cards were used to control weaving patterns. Jacquard's invention served as one of the bases for all future computer developments worldwide. Technological developments in the production of textiles became more and more sophisticated over time and were integrated into all phases of manufacture from analysis of incoming bales of fiber to yarn spinning, knitting, weaving, and dying and finishing.

Acceptance of the New Technology

In the early years of CAD technology, response from the apparel industry to the new electronic directions for production was mixed. First of all, the cost of buying these systems was exorbitant, especially for the smaller companies. The average cost of a Gerber grading and markermaking system was between $250,000 and $350,000.

Of equal importance was the issue of retraining employees and employees' resistance to being retrained. Each company open

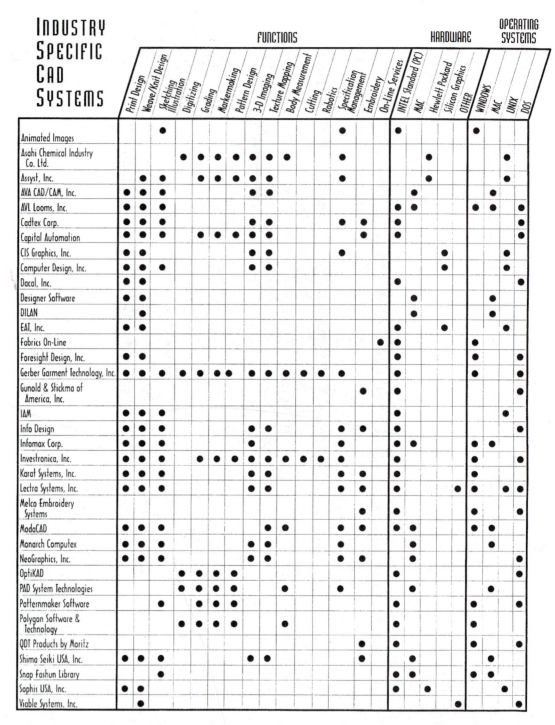

INDUSTRY SPECIFIC CAD SYSTEMS	Print Design	Weave/Knit Design	Sketching/Illustration	Digitizing	Grading	Markermaking	Pattern Design	3-D Imaging	Texture Mapping	Body Measurement	Cutting	Robotics	Specification Management	Embroidery	On-Line Services	INTEL Standard (PC)	Mac	Hewlett Packard	Silicon Graphics	OTHER	WINDOWS	Mac	UNIX	DOS
Animated Images			●										●			●					●			
Asahi Chemical Industry Co. Ltd.				●	●	●	●	●	●	●			●					●					●	
Assyst, Inc.		●	●		●	●	●	●					●					●					●	
AVA CAD/CAM, Inc.	●	●	●					●	●								●					●		
AVL Looms, Inc.	●	●	●													●	●				●	●		●
Cadtex Corp.	●	●	●					●	●				●	●		●								●
Capital Automation	●	●	●		●	●	●	●	●					●		●								●
CIS Graphics, Inc.	●	●						●	●				●						●				●	
Computer Design, Inc.	●	●	●					●	●										●				●	
Dacol, Inc.	●	●														●								●
Designer Software	●	●																●					●	
DILAN		●																●					●	
EAT, Inc.	●	●														●			●				●	
Fabrics On-Line															●	●					●			
Foresight Design, Inc.	●	●														●					●			
Gerber Garment Technology, Inc.	●	●	●	●	●	●	●	●	●	●	●	●	●			●					●			
Gunold & Stickma of America, Inc.														●		●								●
IAM	●	●	●													●							●	
Info Design	●	●	●				●	●					●	●		●								
Infomax Corp.	●	●	●				●						●			●	●				●	●		
Investronica, Inc.	●	●	●		●	●	●	●	●	●	●		●			●								●
Karat Systems, Inc.	●	●	●				●	●					●	●		●					●			
Lectra Systems, Inc.	●	●	●				●	●					●	●		●				●	●		●	●
Melco Embroidery Systems														●		●					●			●
ModaCAD	●	●	●					●	●				●	●		●	●				●	●		
Monarch Computex	●	●	●				●	●					●					●					●	
NeoGraphics, Inc.	●	●	●				●	●					●	●		●								●
OptiKAD				●	●	●	●									●								●
PAD System Technologies				●	●	●	●		●				●					●					●	
Patternmaker Software			●	●	●	●										●					●			●
Polygon Software & Technology				●	●	●	●		●							●					●			
QDT Products by Moritz														●		●					●			●
Shima Seiki USA, Inc.	●	●	●				●	●						●			●						●	
Snap Fashun Library			●													●	●				●	●		
Sophis USA, Inc.	●	●														●		●					●	
Viable Systems, Inc.		●																		●				●

Figure 2–1 CAD system suppliers to the apparel and textile industries (Excerpted from a graphic design by Lee Albright)

to the new technology and able to afford the initial investment would have to redesign the processes and practices that had been in place for years. Patternmakers and markermakers, who often were skilled craftspeople trained under strict European standards, sometimes found the idea of being asked to use a computer more than formidable. Designers often had strong negative reactions to the technology. They felt that images would become standardized and that it took too much time to learn how to operate a system. They thought they could do it better and faster by hand.

Other pressures, however, came to bear on the situation. The U.S. economy was struggling and consumer purchases in the area of soft goods were very low by the end of the 1970s. Goods imported from outside the United States could be sold here at a lower cost than goods we could produce ourselves. Consequently, Americans bought products that were made in other countries and this deflated the economy further. In an effort to get a slice of the pie, U.S. manufacturers began off-shore sourcing, often in third-world countries where costs, especially of labor, were much lower. Fewer and fewer garments were made in the United States; the apparel industry was hit hard and many companies were forced out of business.

The U.S. consumer had a much stronger voice than ever before because discretionary spending dollars were at a low. Retailers and manufacturers wanted to lure those discretionary dollars away by providing the customer with just the right product at just the right price. By the beginning of the 1980s, U.S. consumers had made a strong statement in terms of how they were willing to buy fashion and what they were willing to buy. Fads and dictates were no longer as important or palatable as they had been in the past. The average person either would not or could not buy their fall clothes in July and their spring clothes in February. They wanted to buy their clothing as they needed it throughout a greater part of the season and they wanted it at a good price. Discount stores thrived and large apparel manufacturers began showing new merchandise more often than the traditional two to four seasons a year in order to appeal to the fading fashion customer.

Retailers entered the manufacturing realm on behalf of their customers and their own narrowing profit margins. They felt that they had a better handle on the kind of product that their customer was interested in buying than the **branded** designers and manufacturers did and they developed **private label** programs. In essence, department stores developed their own design teams and in-house labels, and produced the merchandise they needed at a lower price by bypassing the middleman, which in this case was the manufacturer.

Brand name manufacturers, on the other hand, branched out into retail and established their own stores and their own free-standing units within traditional retail outlets. The apparel industry used every creative strategy and mechanism it could come up with to lure the customer into spending.

Quick Response Technology

In a great effort by apparel manufacturers and retailers to rebound and to respond to off-shore production and changing consumerism, **Quick Response Technology (QRT)** was initiated.

Quick Response is a term coined in the early 1970s by Roger Milliken, chairman and CEO of Milliken and Company. As the name implies, Quick Response was designed to respond to market demands within days rather than the months it normally took to order and produce fabric in a mill, then ship it to the garment manufacturer where it was cut and sewn to be shipped again. The goal of Quick Response was to reduce the overall time frame for garment production by establishing communication links among all segments of the process.

Quick Response allowed for smaller inventories of both piece goods and finished goods, faster order processing, smaller mill runs, and smaller cutting and sewing lots. Quick Response sought to connect the retail outlet with the factory electronically, so orders could be passed onto the manufacturer quickly and directly. At the retail level, every sale could be recorded by size, style, and color so the retailer could keep track of stock efficiently and replenish it through direct ordering links with the manufacturer. The result was, of course, much faster turnaround time due in great part to the new CAD technology. This meant that payment was collected more frequently and this created a greater cash-flow situation at each level of manufacture and sales.

Quick Response Technology would not have been possible if the computer technology had not been in place as the primary mechanism for progress. The development of CAD systems in apparel design and production coupled with great advances in inventory tracking and handling allowed QRT to develop.

Many companies bought into the philosophy of QRT, especially those that produced "stock items" such as underwear, men's shirts, and so on. Fashion items were more difficult to organize into the QRT systems because they often change completely before they need to be restocked. Nonetheless, some of the philosophy of QRT, as well as the innovations made by CAD/CAM technology, affected apparel manufacturers at all levels of the industry.

Retailers were also using other electronic mechanisms to keep track of their **stockkeeping units (SKUs)**. The electronic systems were called **electronic data interchange (EDI)** and **merchandise information systems (MIS)**. **Bar coding** also developed as a technology and each piece of merchandise was given a recognizable code bar that identified the manufacturer, size, and so on.

By the end of the 1980s, many manufacturers were using grading and markermaking systems along with business programs for managing inventory control and payroll. Through powerful advertising campaigns and efforts by special interest groups in Washington, consumers began looking for Made in America hang tags on the clothes they purchased. One of the greatest allies in the rebound of the industry at this point was computer technology.

Many apparel industry organizations such as the American Apparel Manufacturers Association (AAMA), Computer Integrated Textile Design Association (CITDA), and Textile Clothing

Technology Corporation [(TC)²] are interested in continuing advances in technological trends. The next step in the evolution of Quick Response is called **flexible manufacturing** or **agile manufacturing**. In these systems, the newest trends in technology, including interactive data exchanges between manufacturing sites, are used to produce small and specific garment lots in a very short time. The goal of the systems is to speed up and customize the manufacturing process so that goods can be brought to market easily and quickly.[5] Technology is available that will cut, sew, or knit a single garment at a time, while keeping costs competitive.

CAD in Today's Fashion Industry

No single aspect of the fashion industry has remained unaffected by the advent of computer technology. By its very nature, fashion is a constantly changing process and if there is any technology that can make that change occur faster and easier, and of course, for less money, that change is adopted.

As we mentioned earlier, the cost of the technology was prohibitive for most designers and manufacturers during the early days. In 1972, the cost of a Gerber system with a workstation with digitizer and plotter for grading and marking was $325,000. In 1995, the price for a more powerful configuration with more advanced features was $30,000-$35,000.[6] As systems have become more affordable, more and more companies have integrated CAD into their work processes. As Walter Wilhelm explained, "A 1972 market study by Camsco, Hughes Aircraft, and Kurt Salmon Associates projected the total CAD market in the apparel industry at less than 50 companies worldwide. Today, there are 20,000 companies using CAD systems."[7]

It is important to mention that in the early years most CAD systems were **proprietary**; that is, the hardware and software were both designed and developed by the CAD company. As the technology evolved, the trend was to use Hewlett Packard, IBM, and Macintosh hardware and to develop the software only. This made it feasible for smaller companies to afford the technology and to use it on computers they already owned. Today, we still have a combination of both methodologies: Some companies offer software that requires proprietary hardware; others are adaptable to common hardware. There are advantages and disadvantages to each, and apparel manufacturers have to decide for themselves, often with the aid of a CAD consultant, which option works best for their particular needs. Many relatively inexpensive off-the-shelf graphics programs can also be used by computer-savvy apparel designers and manufacturers.

One of the critical issues for clothing manufacturers buying CAD systems is that of **interconnectivity**. The systems they buy must have the capacity to be integrated with systems they already own or may plan to own in the future. Additionally, they need to know that their systems can be linked to others worldwide. The AAMA has established standards or parameters that each supplier of CAD technology for patternmaking functions could abide by so that this outcome could be ensured. CITDA is establishing standards for the graphics segment of CAD.

CAD suppliers are responding to the issue of interconnectivity by constructing expandable systems that can be connected with a variety of hardware set-ups and which will accommodate information created by many different types of software. Difficulties arise because suppliers believe that competition in the marketplace will be affected by this standardization. In other words, if all of the CAD systems can be interconnected, what would lure a manufacturer into buying any one particular system?

TYPES OF CAD SYSTEMS

As we mentioned in the introduction, the term *computer-aided design* has become a catch-all for many different types of computer systems used in apparel design and production, some of which have little to do with design in its pure sense. Data management and entry systems for the merchandising and retailing segment of the industry that contain small sketches of garment styles are included under the CAD umbrella. Of course, areas such as patternmaking and grading are called computer-aided *design*, even though making and grading a pattern may not be called "design" by someone who is sketching and creating fabrics for garments. Rather than try to restrict the expansiveness of the definition of CAD, we will continue to use a loose definition here: computer systems involved in the development and manufacture of textiles and apparel.

The number of companies that produce CAD systems has grown each year. From the basic five that sprang up in the early 1970s, Bobbin Magazine surveys list over 30.[8] It is important to be familiar with the names of current CAD suppliers and to attend CAD trade shows held in various parts of the country in order to stay abreast of the technology. A listing of some of the trade shows and exhibitions appears in Figure 2–2.

In the next sections, the types of CAD systems available in today's marketplace will be identified without reference to their company names. Refer to Figure 2–1 for a listing of the names of the suppliers as well as a listing of the functions offered by their CAD systems. The major functions offered by these systems will be isolated and discussed in the upcoming sections. You should note, however, that many suppliers have offices in New York and other large cities and offer private demonstrations of their products to students and faculty by appointment. Other sophisticated systems are available in countries besides the United States and are sometimes on exhibit at the U.S. CAD shows.

**Trade Shows and Exhibitions of CAD Products
for Textiles and Apparel
in the United States**

Yarn Fair International and CAD Expo
    Sheraton New York Hotel and Towers
    contact: National Knitwear and Sportswear Association
    212-683-7520
        September

The Bobbin Show
    Georgia World Congress Center, Atlanta
    contact: Hardy Katz
    305-893-8771
        September

Los Angeles International Textile Show
    California Mart, Los Angeles
    contact: California Mart
        April and October

IFFE International Fashion Fabric Exhibition
    Jacob K. Javitz Convention Center, New York
    contact: The Larkin Group
    1-800-8NY-Show
        April and October

CITDA Computer Integrated Textile Design Association
    Joesph S. Koury Convention Center, Greensboro, NC
    contact: CITDA
    PO Box 849
    Burlington, NC 27216
        June

Figure 2–2   Trade shows and exhibitions of CAD products for the textiles and apparel industries in the United States (dates may vary)

Textile Design Systems

Systems for the design of **woven textiles** are used by designers and merchandisers in many different markets from fabrics for home furnishings to mens-, womens- and childrenswear. Most fabrics, whether yarn dyes, plain weaves, jacquards, or dobbies, are designed using a CAD system for textiles. Printed or flocked fabrics and embroideries are also developed at CAD workstations. The designers can be employed by a manufacturer, design house, private label manufacturer, service company, or textile producer. Some CAD systems are owned by freelance textile designers who work with various apparel companies. In most markets, wherever there are textiles, a computer-aided design system had something to do with the product.

Some textile design programs contain all of the technical information required for weaving, or the entire peg plan, including the yarn type and size and the number of ends and picks for a designated weave. Figure 2–3 shows a printout of binary data that a loom connected to a CAD system uses to weave a two-color design. Other systems simulate the appearance of the woven fabric without the technical data required by the mill.

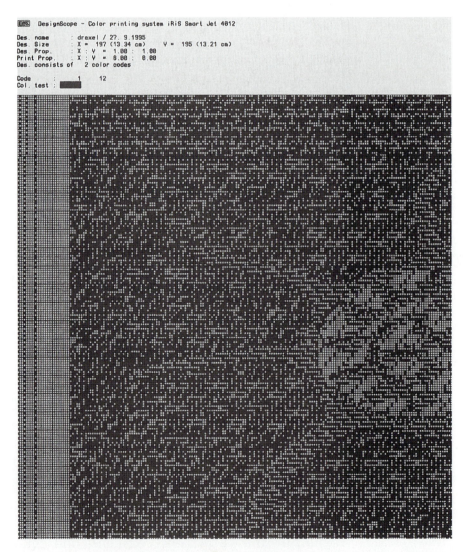

Figure 2–3 A design that has been converted into binary data so that the loom can "read" the information for weaving (Courtesy of EAT, Inc., The DesignScope® Company)

Knitted fabrics   Textile design software is also used to create and modify all types of knitted fabrics and garment parts (see Figure 2–4). Some systems specialize in knitwear production and the final knitted fabric design can be viewed on screen with indications of all stitch formation. The fabric for cut and sew garments or the complete garment for full fashioned pieces can quickly be graphed based on machine gauge and then connected to a knitting machine for production. A CAD knit program will produce a sweater graph that will also include information indicating the amount of yarn needed by color for each top, sweater, and so on.

Printed fabrics   When prints are created, either for wovens or knits, the process usually begins with either original, scanned, or video-input artwork. This process will be discussed in more detail in Chapter 3, but basically, design involves the development and manipulation of a **motif**. The motif can then be resized, recolored, rotated, or multiplied depending on the designer's goal. The arrangement is put into a repeat with the help of the computer. Another option is to start with an existing print or a painting of a print. This is scanned into the computer and color-reduced. Textures and/or weave structures can be indicated so that the printout either on paper or on actual fabric looks very much the way the final product will look (see Plate 1). The textile design system can then show **colorways** in an instant rather than taking the hours needed for hand painting.

It is important to note that color matching the original artwork or fabric, the screen, and the printed output has been a challenge that software developers have been addressing. The technology is improving constantly and many textile design systems now have built-in software that tries to match swatch color to screen color to printer color automatically.

Technical systems allow engravers to create color separations from the CAD-generated image and output them right to film for textile printing processes. These are often referred to as **preproduction textile design systems**. Some voices in the industry predict that engraving and current color separation procedures for printing will soon become outmoded. Complete digital fabric printing is expected to become a commercially viable process in the next few years. Ultimately, this means that manufacturers could buy **greige goods** and do their fabric printing in house right from their CAD systems.[9] It also means a great savings in the cost of producing **strike-offs**, which are printed samples that are sent back to the design room for approval before full-scale production begins.

Yarn-dyed fabric   Yarn-dyed fabrics (plaids, stripes, tweeds, etc.) can be created on screen and exact indications of yarn type, color, and weave structure can be fed into the computer. New yarn types can be designed along with novelty weaves (see Plate 2). Modifications to existing plaids and stripes can be made by the

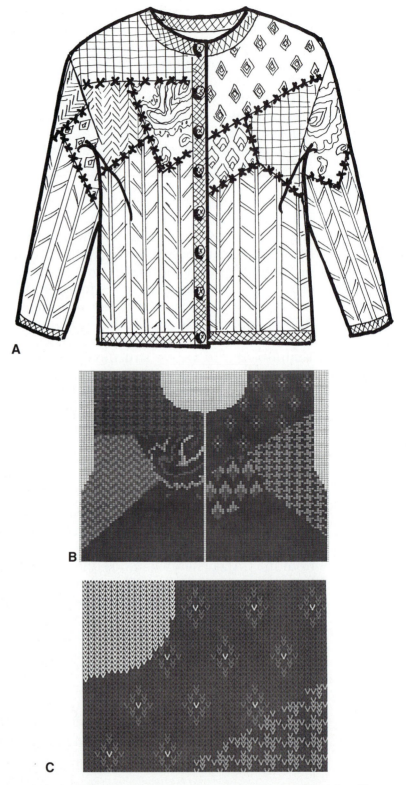

Figure 2–4 (a) Flat sweater rendering with patchwork effects and hand embroidery (b) Sweater graph created with Monarch Design Studio™ software by Monarch Computex (c) Left front detail of knit stitch simulation created in Monarch Design Studio™ (Courtesy of Susan Bourget for Herman Geist © 1995. All rights reserved.)

computer by reproportioning various elements. All of the changes can be printed out for viewing and editing which often eliminates the costs associated with ordering samples from the mill. These systems may also have the preproduction capacity to be linked to a mill for production (see Figure 2–5).

Sophisticated systems that generate dobby and jacquard weaves have existed for many years (see Plate 3). Today's systems drive weaving looms and produce either samples or yardage for production. **Blankets** or **hand looms** are the terms used to refer to the samples created for review and approval.

Figure 2–5 (a) Technical simulation of a dobby weave structure created in ColorWeave© by AVL (Courtesy of AVL Looms, Inc.)

(continued)

Weave	
Design	
Collection	Jackson Mills
Finishing	
Colorway	•

Remarks (Warp):

Date   28 September 95

Composition	
%	**Material**
1	COTON

Weight Yl	
Weight	

Threading	
Warp color	
672A	

	No. of Ends			Yarn code	
	Beam	**Beam**	**Weight**	**Mat.**	**Col.**
A	2754				
B					
C					
D					
E					
F					
G					
H					
I					
J					
K					
L					
M					
N					
O					
P					

Shaft	Heddle
01	185
02	184
03	184
04	185
05	84
06	84
07	84
08	84
09	84
10	84
11	84
12	84
13	168
14	168
15	168
16	168
17	84
18	84

#. shafts	24
Ends/dt	2
Dents/inc	25.50
Ends/inch	51.00
Reed	54.03
Raw width	54.03
Table	

	Thread.	Warp	Dents
Repeat	4	4	4
of	672	672	336
over			
sel. left	33	33	17
sel. right	33	33	17
Fabric	2754	2754	1378

Pegplan	JFF#34
Weft color	
10A4B20A4C20A4D10A	

		Yarn code	
	Weigh	**Mat.**	**Col.**
A	60		
B	4		
C	4		
D	4		
E			
F			
G			
H			

Picks/inch	50.00

	Pegplan	We. col.
Repeat	48	72

Remarks (Weft):

Figure 2–5   (b) Specifications sheet for the fabric (Courtesy of AVL Looms, Inc.)

Fabric		Date	28 September 95
Collection	Jackson Mills		
Design			Colorway

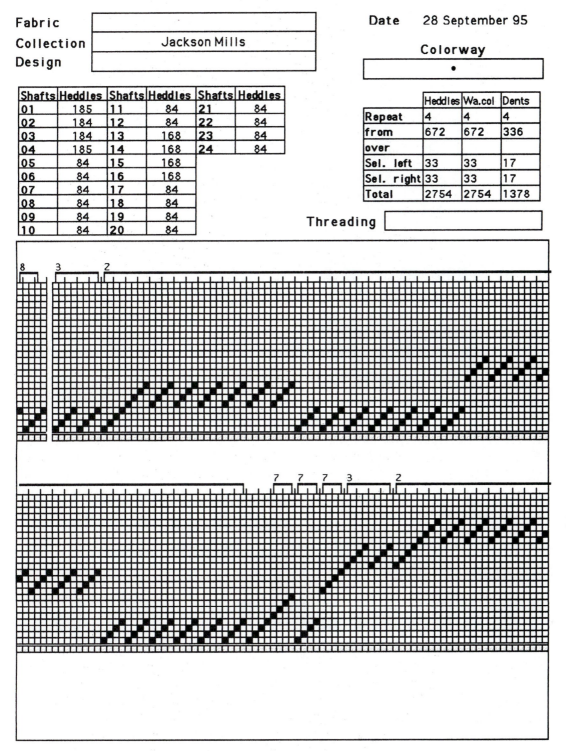

Shafts	Heddles	Shafts	Heddles	Shafts	Heddles
01	185	11	84	21	84
02	184	12	84	22	84
03	184	13	168	23	84
04	185	14	168	24	84
05	84	15	168		
06	84	16	168		
07	84	17	84		
08	84	18	84		
09	84	19	84		
10	84	20	84		

	Heddles	Wa.col	Dents
Repeat	4	4	4
from	672	672	336
over			
Sel. left	33	33	17
Sel. right	33	33	17
Total	2754	2754	1378

Threading

Figure 2–5 (c) Threading diagram shows a single color warp (Courtesy of AVL Looms, Inc.)

(continued)

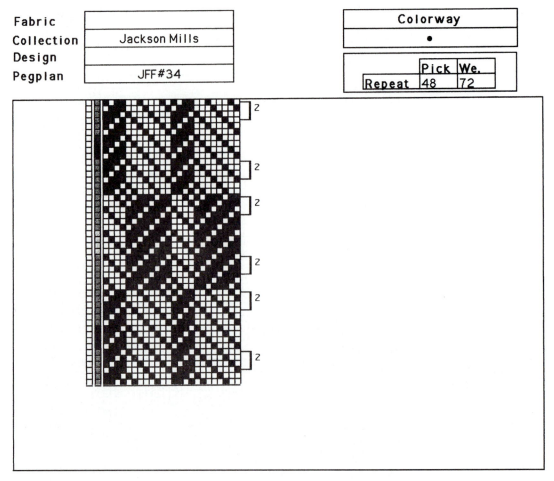

Fabric		Colorway		
Collection	Jackson Mills	•		
Design			Pick	We.
Pegplan	JFF#34	Repeat	48	72

Figure 2–5   (d) The peg plan, or weave diagram, created in the Colorado© Textile Design System by AVL (Courtesy of AVL Looms, Inc.)

Illustration/Sketchpad Systems

These are graphics programs that allow the designer to use a pen or stylus on an electronic pad or large format easel or tablet (see Figure 2–6). Drawings are freehand images which are then stored in the computer. The tendency in current technology is to simulate the illustrator's tactile drawing experience as much as possible by providing a large working area and brushstrokes that offer sensitivity to pressure and simulated line quality. In this way, a designer can produce stylized illustrations that are similar to those drawn on paper with a pen or marker.

Sketchpad systems also help to produce **flat line renderings** and technical drawings of new designs. Often, libraries of flats are either developed or purchased for the designer to work with and alternate between painting and drawing tools. Initially, a designer may develop a personal library by scanning flat drawings into the computer and then manipulating them. Different knit and weave simulations can also be stored in a library and imposed

Figure 2–6 Graphic Instinct™ drawing table (Courtesy of Lectra/ Systèmes, Inc.)

over the sketch to show texture and dimension. Ideas for **silhouettes** can also be stored in a library and used as needed.

Flats and illustrations can be filled with fabric designed on a textile design system and then shown in all of the projected colorways for a season (see Figure 2–7). These systems can be used to develop storyboards, line presentations, and many other sales and communications tools.

Texture Mapping: 2½- and 3-D Draping Software

This technology allows for the visualization of fabric on a body. **Texture mapping** is the process by which fabric can be draped over a form in a realistic way. This means, for example, that if the fabric is a stripe, the mapping will produce an image in which the stripe curves around the body, or bends with the elbow, or rolls over the flare of a skirt. In other words, the pattern of the cloth is

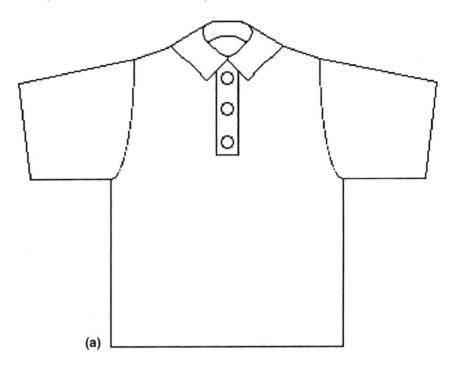

(a)

(b)

Figure 2–7 (a) Computer generated flat line rendering; (b) Flat filled with textile design using CLARIS™ painting and drawing programs.

contoured to match the form underneath it. Both 2½-D and 3-D systems rely on texture mapping technology.

In 2½-D imaging, the designer starts with an image of a model wearing a garment (see Figure 2–8). This is usually a photograph that has been scanned into the computer. Each section of the garment is outlined from seam line to seam line and/or hemline. Then a swatch of new fabric created in the textile design system is laid over the area and the computer automatically fills in the area with the new color or pattern. All of the folds and shadows in the original garment are maintained. Most systems have separate lighting controls so that the designer can enhance the folds and shadows in the image. The result is the original silhouette worn by the original model in a new fabric (see Figure 2–9).

Three-D draping systems allow the designer to see the garment from any angle with the aid of 3-D glasses. "The designer can reach under a sleeve, for example, to adjust a cuff without having to rotate the model!"[10] These systems can also be used to drape flat patterns onto a form for fit and visualization. Conversely, developments are under way for a 3-D image to be flattened into a 2-D pattern. This has been accomplished successfully using stretch fabrics and research is ongoing to include fabrics of all weights and constructions.

These 3-D systems are used widely in the automobile industry and in furniture and home furnishings as well as footwear because the objects to be draped over are stable in size. Bodies are more troublesome because they vary so greatly in size and form. Additionally, the quality, weight, and drapability of the fabric itself is so variable that it is difficult to include these variables in the design of a software program.

All of this technology has had a dramatic impact on a designer's ability to test his or her ideas. If a new garment can be simulated on screen in minutes, then the time-consuming task of developing samples is greatly reduced. Catalogues and brochures, along with many other types of sales, advertising, and marketing tools, can be developed without investing in samplemaking, hiring models, and taking photographs. The technology allows for **virtual imaging**, which simply means that a real product or sample does not exist. Lands' End, a well-known catalogue company, used a **virtual product** on the cover of its July 1995 catalogue (see Plate 30). In this way, they were able to test consumer response to a product without ever having created a "real" sample!

Embroidery Systems

Designers who work with embroidered designs and motifs can create original artwork on the computer or use scanned images of designs. The design is outlined section by section and stitch types and colors are assigned. This data is then fed into an embroidery machine with one or multiple heads for stitching (see Figure 2–10).

Figure 2–8   Original photograph of model

Specifications and Costing Systems

These systems store all style information including a flat sketch, size specifications, trim requirements, and size grade charts. These documents are called **specifications sheets** or **spec sheets**. They keep track of all information pertinent to the design and production of a style including folding and shipping instructions if necessary. Figure 2–11 is an example of one type of spec sheet, but it is important to note that each company designs its own documents for in-house use, so spec sheets are not standardized throughout the industry. Spec and costing systems help to ensure accuracy and consistency when a company has a number of production sites, and are particularly helpful and even mandatory when a portion of the work is done overseas. Most companies have experienced communication problems related to cultural and language barriers and CAD visualizations minimize the risk of misunderstanding.

Specifications management is an extremely important aspect of CAD because it controls all of the paperwork that supports the production, costing, and delivery of the garment. As a designer

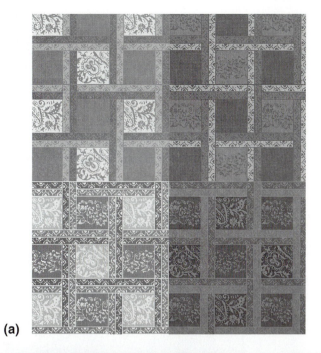

(a)

(b)

Figure 2–9   (a) Textile simulation (b) Texture mapping of one colorway on original photograph (Courtesy of Shima Seiki, USA, Inc.)

Figure 2–10 © Melco embroidery systems (Courtesy of Melco Industries, Inc.)

works on a garment, all of the costs related to that item, even the amount of thread consumption, can be determined immediately. The impact of any slight change in design or in a sewing sequence can be seen immediately. An apparel manufacturer's spec system is usually available on line so that access to information is available to anyone in the company, no matter where they are in the world.

Specifications and costing systems can be linked to inventory control systems as well. They add information from markermaking and preproduction systems and keep track of all data from yard goods and trims to the finished product. EDI systems connecting the mill, the factory, and the retail store expand the information network.

Digitizing Systems

Digitizers input original patterns into the computer for use and storage. An operator places the pattern piece on a digitizing table and uses an instrument with a magnifying glass center and crosshairs representing the X and Y axes. This instrument (the

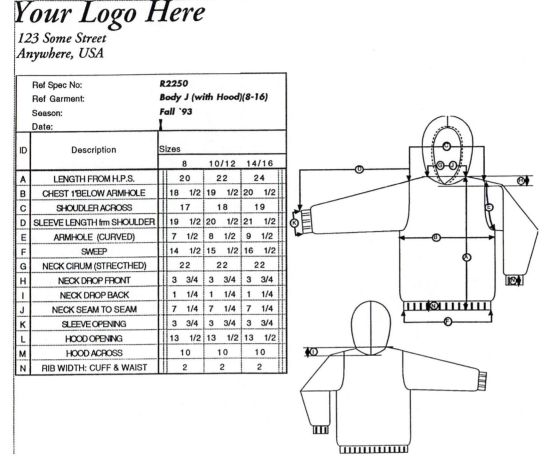

Your Logo Here
123 Some Street
Anywhere, USA

Ref Spec No:	**R2250**			
Ref Garment:	**Body J (with Hood)(8-16)**			
Season:	**Fall '93**			
Date:				

ID	Description	Sizes		
		8	10/12	14/16
A	LENGTH FROM H.P.S.	20	22	24
B	CHEST 1"BELOW ARMHOLE	18 1/2	19 1/2	20 1/2
C	SHOUDLER ACROSS	17	18	19
D	SLEEVE LENGTH frm SHOULDER	19 1/2	20 1/2	21 1/2
E	ARMHOLE (CURVED)	7 1/2	8 1/2	9 1/2
F	SWEEP	14 1/2	15 1/2	16 1/2
G	NECK CIRUM (STRECTHED)	22	22	22
H	NECK DROP FRONT	3 3/4	3 3/4	3 3/4
I	NECK DROP BACK	1 1/4	1 1/4	1 1/4
J	NECK SEAM TO SEAM	7 1/4	7 1/4	7 1/4
K	SLEEVE OPENING	3 3/4	3 3/4	3 3/4
L	HOOD OPENING	13 1/2	13 1/2	13 1/2
M	HOOD ACROSS	10	10	10
N	RIB WIDTH: CUFF & WAIST	2	2	2

Figure 2–11   Specifications sheet created in SpecView® pre-production system (Courtesy of Infomax Corp.)

digitizer) is clicked around the edges and internal lines of the pattern piece and at each click point the X and Y coordinates are recorded by the computer. The computer then connects all the points to create the pattern shape on screen. The operator has a type of keyboard to identify necessary descriptors, such as size, style name or number, and so forth.

Some systems allow the operator to place a hard pattern on a large table-sized tablet and input the pattern shape by tracing around the pattern. Changes to the pattern can be made on this tablet or pad using traditional methods and tools (hip curve and ruler) and the result will come up on the computer screen. Note that large format scanners are also available for pattern input and current technology makes less and less use of traditional digitizing equipment (see Figure 2–12).

Grading Systems

After a sample size pattern has been input, it has to be graded up and down in size. Certain points on the pattern are considered

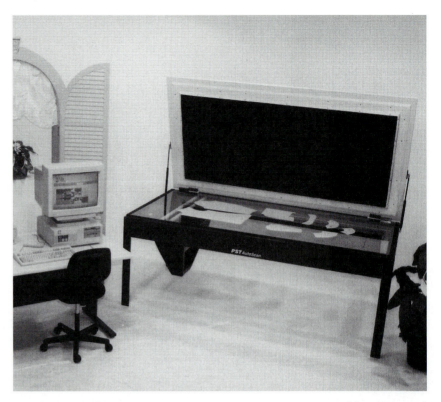

Figure 2–12 Polynest AutoScan pattern-scanning table (Courtesy of Polygon Software and Technology)

"growth points" or places at which the pattern has to be increased or decreased to accommodate changing body size. At each growth point, the operator indicates a grade rule to the computer. This grade rule lets the system know which way to move on the X and Y coordinates in order to increase or decrease size. The system will then automatically produce the pattern shapes in all the prespecified sizes. The pattern parts can then be placed one inside another, or **nested**, from smallest to largest so that the patternmaker can pick up any problems with the grade at a glance (see Figure 2–13).

Markermaking Systems

A marker is the arrangement of all the pattern parts for a particular style in the optimal configuration for maximum fabric utilization. In marketmaking systems, the patterns in all graded sizes appear on the screen in small scale and the operator moves them around until the least percentage of fabric waste is achieved (see Figure 2–14). Each pattern size appears in a different color to avoid confusion. The system will let the operator know the percentage of waste by command. Some systems use algorithms to compute pattern arrangement and the operator's involvement is minimized. Width parameters of the fabric are taken into account as are any

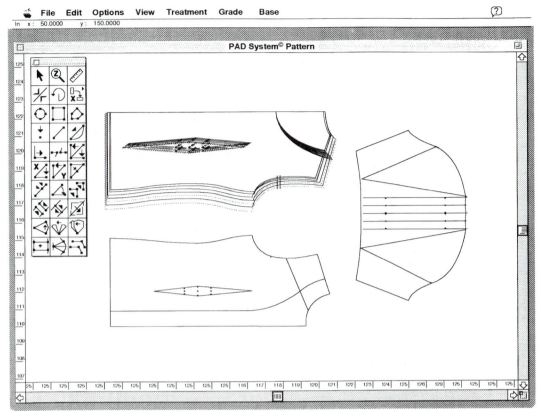

Figure 2-13   Nested bodice back pattern (Courtesy of PAD System©
Technologies)

stripe or plaid lines and nap considerations. Automatic matching
of stripes and plaids is common to most systems. If the operator
wants to rotate the patterns by degree to allow them to be squeezed
on more tightly, this can be accomplished easily.

Plotting functions are linked to markermaking systems and
allow the marker to be printed in varying scales on large rolls of
continuous paper. The paper is then overlaid on the stacked fabric prior to cutting. Individual patterns in full scale or half scale as
well as nested patterns can be printed out using the plotter (see
Figure 2–15).

Cutting operations   are connected to markermaking systems
and calculate the number of layers (plies) of fabric that have to
be cut to accommodate orders for color and size in a particular
style (see Figure 2–16). Cutting systems can be used without plotting out the marker, but rather by passing along the information
about pattern shapes generated by the markermaking system
directly to an automated cutting machine. The cutting machine
operates on its own without being pushed by a human being. **Cut
paths** for the machine to follow can also be calculated by the
computer for the most efficient and accurate results.

Figure 2-14 AssyCam markermaking system (Courtesy of Assyst, Inc.)

Pattern Design Software (PDS)

Patterns, blocks, or **slopers** that are stored in the computer can be manipulated by the operator using most of the same flat pattern techniques used in the hand-drafting methods. All of the time-consuming pattern manipulations such as pivoting darts, adding flare, and adding pleats can be done quickly using functions and tools similar to those found in drafting and drawing programs. Although the blocks or slopers are originally fed into the system by way of digitizing or scanning, subsequent new patterns can be created from stored parts, thus greatly reducing the time needed to draft original patterns. The samplemaking process is also reduced in time and cost because the patterns stored in the systems have already been tested for fit and accuracy (see Figure 2–17).

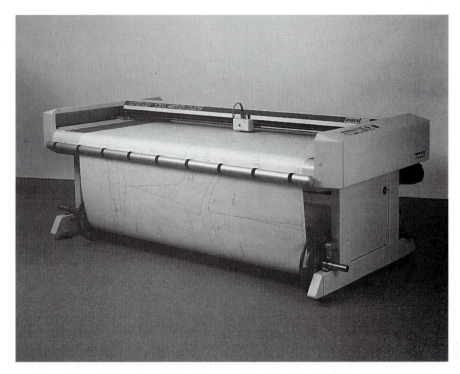

Figure 2–15   "Wild Tasoo" plotter and pattern cutter (Courtesy of the Zund Corporation)

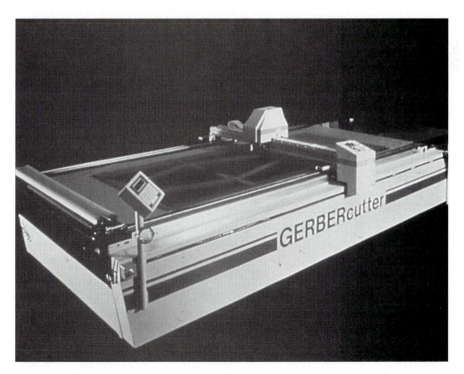

Figure 2–16   GerberCutter® Machine (Courtesy of Gerber Garment Technology, Inc.)

Figure 2–17 Invesmark pattern design system (Courtesy of Investronica, Inc.)

Pattern generation software (PGS)   Pattern generation software is pattern design software that operates in a question-and-answer format. Rather than drafting a new collar on a shirt using drawing tools, the patternmaker uses word and measurement commands to modify the style on the screen. Many different garment components are stored in the system and the designer can combine and alter the parts to conform to the sketch. For example, Bodice Front and Back X can be called up and combined with Sleeve Y and Collar Z. If the shoulder seam needs reduction, the operator can tell the computer to reduce by 0.5 inches and the computer will not only reduce the bodice pieces, but it will also make the appropriate adjustments to the sleeve and collar. Here again, fit has already been tested on all of the stored pattern parts, so samplemaking procedures can be shortened or eliminated. After the pattern has been completed for the new design, the computer can generate a complete set of graded patterns in all sizes.

Body measurement software   Body measurement software uses specific individual measurements to modify a stored pattern and produce a new one that is particular to a single customer. Sometimes the customer's measurements at certain body points are fed into the system which then makes adjustments at matching points on the pattern. In other cases, a video image of the customer wearing a body stocking is used and the computer generates an image of the person and uses pattern generation software to convert measurements from the image to a specific pattern. These systems are used for tailored garments, perfect fit jeans, and by businesses that offer custom fitting. Another type of system that can be used for patternmaking and fitting allows for input of the dress form or mannequin (see Figure 2–18). The computer can then lay the pattern parts over the form to see a simulation of the final garment. Matching of plaids and stripes and placement of pattern can be manipulated and visualized.

A new trend in customizing clothing includes technology called **electronic body scanning**. After being scanned, each customer would have a personal "smart card" "which would make their measurements portable so consumers could use them from store to store, for catalogue shopping, etc."[11] When linked with the concept of agile manufacturing discussed earlier in this chapter, consumers could hope for a future attuned to customization and personalization of their apparel needs.

Figure 2–18 AGMS 3-D product design system (Courtesy of Asahi Chemical Industry Co. Ltd.)

Robotics and Garment-Moving Technology

In a factory, conveyer systems can be set up to move cut pieces among sewing machine operators until the full garment is assembled (see Figure 2–19). An overhead line system holds clipped garment parts together and each operator performs his or her function. The parts then continue on to the next operator until the piece is fully assembled. Computerized sewing machines are used in many operations in which a specified number of stitches in a particular direction or series of directions can be preprogrammed.

Commercial Software Systems

Software such as Adobe Photoshop™, Adobe Illustrator®, and many other commercially available graphics and paint programs are used by many companies to achieve specific goals, such as catalogue development, and as a supplement to proprietary sys-

Figure 2–19 GerberMover® conveyer system for garment production (Courtesy of Gerber Garment Technology, Inc.)

tems they may own already. Some companies have come up with libraries either on disk or on CD ROM that an apparel manufacturer might purchase. These libraries contain hundreds of flat drawings or illustrations, historic costume examples, textile prints, and weaves or knit stitches.

Commercial patternmaking software is available for PCs and Macs that allows a small manufacturer or home or school user to create and modify patterns.

STUDY QUESTIONS AND PROBLEMS

1. Select two CAD vendors from Figure 2–1. Make sure both companies offer sketch or illustration components. Request brochures from these companies and compare the design tools of the two systems.
2. Research the private label names and products in your local department stores. Which branded labels do they compete with? How do the prices of the products compare?
3. Discuss the positive and negative effects of using virtual products in mail order catalogues.
4. Create a graph and use it to compare the tools of two off-the-shelf drawing or painting programs. Which do you think would serve better as a program for a fashion designer? Why?

Chapter **3**

From Sketch to Market: How CAD Systems Are Used

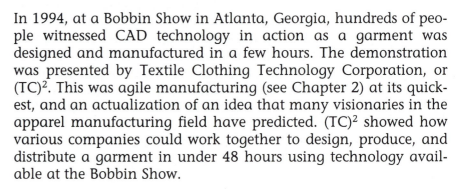

In 1994, at a Bobbin Show in Atlanta, Georgia, hundreds of people witnessed CAD technology in action as a garment was designed and manufactured in a few hours. The demonstration was presented by Textile Clothing Technology Corporation, or (TC)². This was agile manufacturing (see Chapter 2) at its quickest, and an actualization of an idea that many visionaries in the apparel manufacturing field have predicted. (TC)² showed how various companies could work together to design, produce, and distribute a garment in under 48 hours using technology available at the Bobbin Show.

The real time demonstration used a woman's top and skirt pattern in cotton and polyester base fabric, on which print modifications were made and communicated electronically. Through a video link, a buyer at J.C. Penney in Dallas requested a modification in a print from a designer at FIT in New York. Through 3-D computer design, the buyer could see the revised garment from all perspectives.

The new approved print pattern was communicated electronically to a booth at the Bobbin Show where in-store merchandising materials, such as posters, banners and hangtags, were produced automatically by Cactus, a digital printing company.

The white base fabric was then sent to Gerber cutter, an automatic screenprinting area, and on to be assembled by modular manufacturing stations at the Juki and Sunbrand booths.

An audience participant entered a personal order with size and color specifications for a garment and received a bar coded receipt that could be used to track the status of the garment during all stages of production. The final product was sent to a distribution point on the Bobbin exhibition floor.[12]

Traditionally, clothing goes through three basic processes on the road from sketch to hanger: design, production, and merchandising (not necessarily in that order). There is a great deal of overlap when it comes to defining design, merchandising, and production as three separate entities. For example, the professional who works on a computer to generate new patterns is often called a designer. During the early years of CAD technology, all pattern-making processes were called design processes. And many CAD suppliers still refer to these functions as design functions.

Very often a merchandiser is responsible for putting together a group of silhouettes for a private label program. Once again, terminology becomes an issue and the differentiation between design and merchandising becomes blurred. Increasingly, roles and job responsibilities are merging and blending, often in direct relation to the size of the company or simply because each particular company has its own methods and practices. Each manufacturing and/or design firm establishes its own job descriptions and parameters. Ultimately, no matter what the job title or description, employees work together to meet the goals established by their company. In order to realize those goals, each employee becomes part of a chain or a flexible, information-sharing network. An illustration of the various job functions and the way information and decisions in the process can be shared is illustrated in Figure 3–1. Again, there are no hard and fast rules; each company divides job responsibilities to best fit its needs.

As job descriptions broaden and differentiation among merchandising, design, and production becomes more difficult, teamwork among employees and interconnectivity among computers takes priority. Rather than trying to study the process under old job titles, it may be more helpful to look at the entire process under more open-ended divisions. These divisions will include design, merchandising, and production practices but will not restrict job functions by labeling. These basic divisions are: conceptualization, definition, preproduction, production, and promotion. These will each be defined and described in terms of the CAD assistance used at each stage.

CONCEPTUALIZATION

Conceptualization is the idea, the vision, or the spirit of the clothes that are yet to be made. It is established in the imaginations of designers and merchandisers and is informed and influenced by forecasting services, the worlds of art and entertainment, politics, and social mores. Everything in the great environment surrounding us is inspirational in one way or another because it demands some kind of human response. All the CAD programs in the world could not help a design and merchandising team come up with a concept for a new season. The computer can be used as a notebook to record predicted colors and silhouettes or as a storage system for

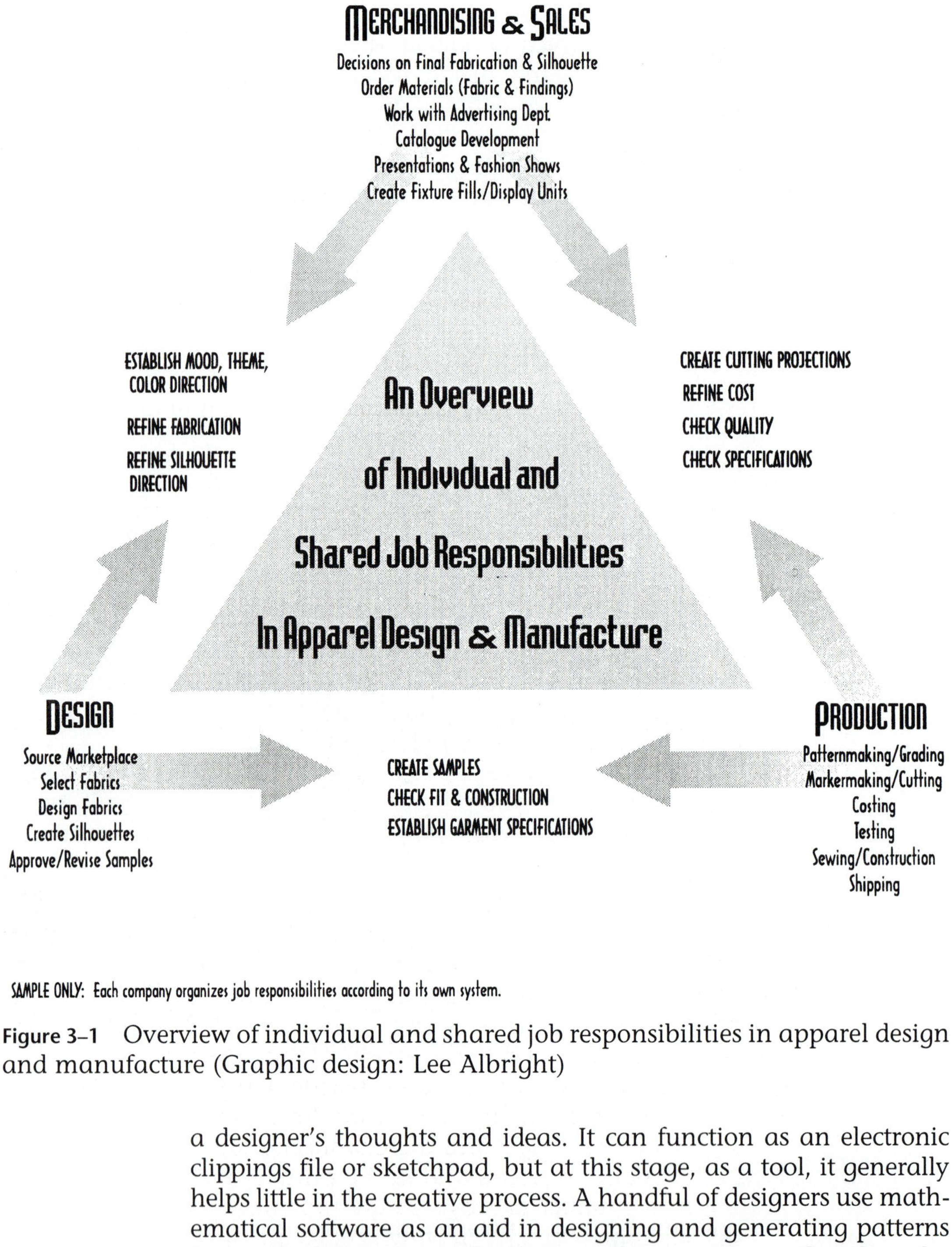

MERCHANDISING & SALES

Decisions on Final Fabrication & Silhouette
Order Materials (Fabric & Findings)
Work with Advertising Dept.
Catalogue Development
Presentations & Fashion Shows
Create Fixture Fills/Display Units

An Overview

of Individual and

Shared Job Responsibilities

In Apparel Design & Manufacture

ESTABLISH MOOD, THEME,
COLOR DIRECTION

REFINE FABRICATION

REFINE SILHOUETTE
DIRECTION

CREATE CUTTING PROJECTIONS

REFINE COST

CHECK QUALITY

CHECK SPECIFICATIONS

DESIGN

Source Marketplace
Select Fabrics
Design Fabrics
Create Silhouettes
Approve/Revise Samples

CREATE SAMPLES

CHECK FIT & CONSTRUCTION

ESTABLISH GARMENT SPECIFICATIONS

PRODUCTION

Patternmaking/Grading
Markermaking/Cutting
Costing
Testing
Sewing/Construction
Shipping

SAMPLE ONLY: Each company organizes job responsibilities according to its own system.

Figure 3–1   Overview of individual and shared job responsibilities in apparel design and manufacture (Graphic design: Lee Albright)

a designer's thoughts and ideas. It can function as an electronic clippings file or sketchpad, but at this stage, as a tool, it generally helps little in the creative process. A handful of designers use mathematical software as an aid in designing and generating patterns for textile design. Presently, they are the exception rather than the rule (see Jhane Barnes interview, Chapter 6).

The computer is extremely helpful, however, when designers and merchandisers meet to discuss the direction or concept for the upcoming line. Information provided by an inventory control system helps the design team to evaluate their ideas about color and silhouette direction based on past performance. Sales figures from previous seasons will show which colors consumers were most interested in buying. It will show which silhouettes were most popular. It will indicate how successful trendy or novelty items were in relation to the staples. It will answer questions such as: Did our customer like skirts last season or did she prefer pants? Did she prefer an 18-inch-length skirt or a 20-inch length?

The conceptualization process involves discussion and exchange of ideas among members of a design team. Designers expand, elaborate, and creatively resolve the company's new direction for a season. They play with ideas and set parameters for the definition of the line based on customer needs, trends for the future, and the spirit of the company.

DEFINITION

Once a commitment to the direction of the line has been established, mood and color are finalized. The mood is illustrated through **swipes** from magazines, postcard images, and other pictorial methods. This overall mood or feeling is organized by the design and merchandising teams. It becomes a visual communication tool that helps marketing and sales understand the seasonal direction for the line. These are usually presented in board format and are called **mood boards** or **concept boards** (see Figure 3–2). For the most part, a CAD system is not required at this stage, but often the components for these boards are scanned into the computer and either a textile design system or a graphics program is used to organize and work with the images. Yarns, paint chips, and fabric swatches can be scanned in to illustrate the color palette, or color tabs can be generated right from the computer to describe the seasonal palette.

As the line is divided into groups, each group is given a theme, which is also illustrated pictorially and assigned a certain portion of the palette. These are called **theme boards** and provide more specific direction for the clothing than the mood board. (This will be discussed in greater detail in Chapter 4.) Once a theme for a group is established, fabric design and selection begin.

A textile designer will use a **textile design system** to create the fabrics for the group and/or the line. First, the color palette selected by the design and merchandising team will have to be matched both on screen and in the printing process. This can be done in a number of ways: many programs use the PANTONE TEXTILE Color System®* in which colors are matched by numbers based on hue, value, and brightness. Once the palette is established using these numbers, the information can be transmitted on any connected CAD system from the design room through production at the textile or knitting mill.

One of the greatest problems CAD designers have experienced in the last few years lies in color matching; that is, the color

---

*All trademarks noted herein are either the property of Pantone, Inc. or their respective companies.

Figure 3–2   This mood board presents color direction for the active sportswear market (Courtesy of Cotton Incorporated)

illuminated on the terminal is rarely the color that matches a designer's swatch or the color that is produced by the printer. Some designers use instruments called **spectrophotometers** and **colorimeters** to measure color so that it can be accurately matched to screen and printing processes. Other systems have color conversion software installed as part of the CAD software. The oldest, and until very recently the most accurate, methods have been to do all of the matching by eye. This is a painstaking process and requires that the designer be able to work with colors that may look incorrect on screen, but may be acceptable when printed. The CAD industry has been hard at work trying to resolve color difficulties and limitations, and color matching systems are becoming available that promise to correct the problems.

A recent development in CAD technology provides the designer with an instant dye recipe for any color that he or she selects. This recipe is a formula for mixing colors that is attached to the textile design as it goes through to production. This system offers accurate color matching between the computer generated design and the dye house.

Currently, there is a strong trend among CAD designers to use a scanner to input art for textile design. Great care must be taken to ensure that the images used are copyright free or that the designer has obtained the rights to the art from the proper sources. Piracy is illegal and should be rejected.

Often, a painting or a swatch of printed fabric will be scanned into the computer. The image can then be manipulated in many ways. The designer can capture a single motif from the pictorial image and the software can help to create the **repeat** pattern for the designer to see. The color arrangement of the image can be changed completely to all new colors if so desired; but first, concern has to be given to the number of colors in the scan.

When an image or a piece of fabric is scanned into the computer, it may be read by the computer to have hundreds or thousands of colors. This happens partly because of the way the scanner reads light reflected from the surface of the fabric, and partly because colors blended in a painting produce many similar, but different hues (see Plate 4a). Since producing fabrics in hundreds of colors is usually undesirable because of the cost involved, the designer has to use the **color reduction** capabilities of the software. The computer can reduce to a certain number of colors automatically. For example, the designer can ask that the computer reduce from 300 colors to seven colors. The computer will automatically choose those seven colors that appear in the image most frequently by percentage. This often leads to a great deal of lost detail and depth, but it is possible that the effect is desirable in certain instances. The designer can choose to protect certain colors that he or she feels are important to the integrity of the print and let the computer select the rest based on percentage. Or the designer can manually select the colors that he or she wishes to keep. The computer will then remove the remaining colors from the image. Color reduction is an important skill that a CAD designer must develop if he or she is working from a scanned image (see Plate 4b).

Once the image has been color reduced, the edges can be cleaned up and it can be recolored according to the palette that has been chosen for the season. CAD allows the designer many options in working with the print. It can be resized, combinations of resized motifs can be put together, the print can be laid over a new background pattern, and on and on. The possibilities are endless; very often, the unplanned, happy accidents lead to exciting results.

Print motifs and repeats for printed fabric can also be designed from scratch rather than from existing prints. A designer might work in a freehand way to create fabric. Painting and drawing tools can be used to develop an original motif on screen and then the textile design program can be used to show the motif in repeat as a straight drop, half drop, quarter drop, and so on (see Plate 4c).

Next, the designer will probably need to show the new print in a number of different colorways (see Plate 5a,b,c). The colorways can be generated in an instant and this represents a great savings in cost to the apparel company because traditional methods required that an artist be hired to paint the recolorings by hand. Hand painting a new colorway can take hours and can become quite expensive. Many design systems will automatically show every possible sequence and combination of selected colors in a print for the designer to edit. As a result, the designer doesn't even have to take the time to recolor a print one color at a time, because the CAD system will show every possibility and the designer will select those that work best.

The designer can then develop **coordinates**, such as stripes and plaids, and **companion prints** using elements from the original print (see Chapter 6). Since the palette is already available, a simple function will produce an image of a stripe. The designer selects the specific colors and the width of each stripe and the computer creates the image and puts it into a repeat, if commanded to do so. Plates 6, 7, and 8 show coordinated prints based on the original theme.

Plaid generation is more complicated because when two different colors are woven together, a new color is created. Textile design systems can automatically generate this new color. The designer can also specify the type and width of yarn used in the warp and weft as well as design his or her own yarns. The **warp** and **weft** are referred to as **ends** and **picks** by professionals in the textile industry. Designers decide on the structure of the weave—whether it is a twill, a satin weave, a plain weave, and so on. The computer will display an image of the woven fabric once all of the commands have been given. Figure 3–3 shows three different two-color weaves as represented by a textile design system—a plain weave, a twill, and a compound tapestry weave.

In the past, visualizing these new fabric ideas meant ordering a **strike-off** or a **blanket** from the mill. Now, the designer can

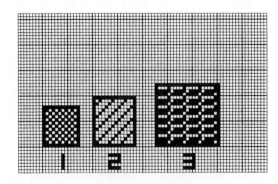

Figure 3–3 (left to right) Peg plan of plain weave, twill weave, and compound tapestry weave (Courtesy of EAT, Inc., The Design-Scope® Company)

print out the new fabric using a high-level Iris or Stork® printer and see the new design printed *on fabric* in minutes. When all final decisions have been made, the information can be sent electronically to the mill for production.

The process for designing knits is similar to that used in woven design. Prints and stripes for piece goods can be assigned a particular yarn type and given a **gauge** based on the knitting machine. The design can be graphed and coded by the computer with instructions for the knitting machine. Various stitch types (cable, pointelle, etc.) can be keyed in and the image can be seen instantly on screen (see Figure 3–4). Full-fashioned knits can also be designed using a similar process. In the past, traditional hand-done **sweater graphing** methods could take hours of a designer's time. The size of the grid on the graph paper indicated the number of stiches per inch and each block represented a stitch. The blocks would be colored in one at a time until the design was finalized.

Sometimes the designer needs to create simple **fabric simulations** on screen without technical production statistics about yarn size, number of ends, and so forth. These simulations are used for presentation purposes only and indicate shading and texture of the fabric without technical specifications for the loom or knitting machine. Libraries are available on CD ROM and disk which contain scans of various textures, weaves, and knit stitches that the designer can apply to a print or a solid fabric.

An **Illustration** or **Sketch Pad System** is used along with the textile design system to make decisions regarding silhouette and line development. In these systems the fabric developed in a textile design program can be integrated with silhouette and construction detail to produce a product line. Often, textile design systems include sketchpad capabilities. Sketch systems allow a designer to work freehand from a scanned-in drawing or from flats and illustrations stored in the library. A designer who works freehand with traditional drawing media can do an illustration on paper and scan the image into the computer for further elaboration. He or she can also trace over an original hand-done illustration using a stylus and a tablet for input to the system. For the most part, sketch/illustration systems allow for a stylized rendering of the product.

Flats or technical drawings can also be done using a sketch/illustration system. Some programs come with disks that contain parts of garments—fronts, backs, sleeves, pockets, and so on—for a designer or merchandiser to assemble and reassemble at will. Figure 3–5 is an example of such a program. Some software includes historical costume sketches and other inspirational resources. Many companies develop their own personal libraries of flats.

The sketch and textile design systems can work together (often they offer similar functions) to show fabric on the silhouette. Many simply fill the illustrations or flat line drawings with pattern for a two-dimensional view of the potential garment, which is similar to the paint bucket function in most graphics pro-

Figure 3–4 CAD-generated sweater designs (Courtesy of Jan Marshall)

grams. These are then used for presentation boards, line boards, sales meetings, catalogues, and in-house records of the upcoming season's merchandise. Some companies take the work done on one of these systems and import it into a desktop publishing program for catalogue development.

CAD-generated fabrics can then be used with a 2½-D or a 3-D simulation program to show the fabric on a body. The systems simulate the way the newly designed fabric would drape on a figure. These images often start with a scanned-in photograph or photo reproduction. The garment fabric that the model in the photograph is wearing is replaced with the newly designed fabric. These are called **texture-mapped** images because the computer creates a "map" of the original garment in the photograph and the new fabric replaces the old, maintaining the folds and drape of the original (see Figure 3–6). The results can be printed out and used on presentation boards to show to a merchandising team or to a customer for a more realistic idea of what the newly designed

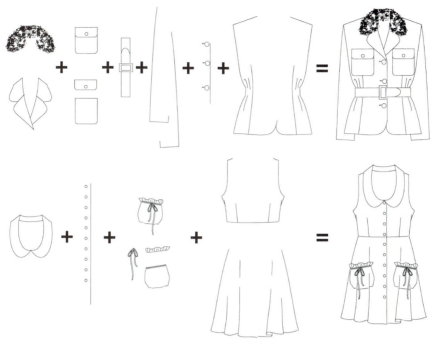

Figure 3–5 Garment parts "snap" together to create the final design (Courtesy of SnapFashun™, Inc.)

Figure 3–6 Texture mapping can eliminate the need for samples to be made in various colors and patterns (Courtesy of Shima Seiki, USA, Inc.)

or recolored fabric will look like on a body. Texture mapping is so descriptive that it is actually used in place of samples. The savings in the cost of making prototypes is quite substantial and makes the return on the investment of a system worthwhile.

Texture mapping is a $2\frac{1}{2}$-D representation. It should not be confused with a 3-D system, which enables the designer to rotate the image in space and view it from all perspectives.

All of the processes described thus far under Definition are interactive: designers, merchandisers, buyers, and sales personnel work together editing new fabrics and new garments. A manufacturer can work with a retail buyer right at the screen to modify product. Changes in color and scale are fast and easy to accomplish. It is a given that technology can now allow product to be developed interactively among teams who work in different cities in different regions of the globe.

Photo credit: Laura Satori

Interview with Craig Stringer
Senior Computer Graphic Designer
GAP

R.W.C.:   How did you get your start in CAD?

Stringer: I graduated from the University of Tennessee in Knoxville. I was taking merchandising but I really wasn't interested in retail. I was really more interested in design. There was an instructor there who was trying to manipulate a basic CAD program for airplane design and use it for patternmaking. I took that class and became interested in how computers were going to be used in the fashion industry and I also applied for an internship situation at FIT. One of the classes I got into involved learning to use a new CAD program that they had there. And while I was working on it, there were a couple of companies that came by to see how FIT was using them (computers) and one of them asked me if I was interested in going to work for them after I finished school. So I went to work for them that January right after I graduated. That was J. G. Hook. Then the Gap bought its (CAD) equipment and I interviewed with the Gap and I came on here. I've been here six years in May.

R.W.C.:   Which CAD system are you using now?

Stringer: This is the CDI Euphoria® Program, which we use mostly for flat representations of plaids and stripes.

R.W.C.:   At this point, do you consider yourself a designer or merchandiser?

Stringer: Oh, we're definitely designers; we work with merchandisers.

R.W.C.:   What are your job responsibilities?

Stringer: What I do is work with all of the designers for men, boys, women, girls, and babies. I help them make their presentations to the merchandisers. They (the designers) are really the creative aspect and I interpret for them. Basically, we have a set palette that is created in the beginning of each season four times a year. They (the designers) present items that they would like to see in different colors. My job is more limited to an actual production-oriented position where I do a lot in a small amount of time. I take what they give me and I print it out as quickly as possible in as many ways as possible. They narrow it down from that. I'm basically an assistant to all the designers at the Gap so it's an interesting position. I do have a lot of hands on with everything that goes in the store. Periodically, when things go in the store, I have a real ability to say, "Well, I really worked with that, or I manipulated that to make it look that way." It's fun.

R.W.C.:   Is the palette selected by the merchandising staff and then handed down to design?

Stringer: No, the design staff creates a specific palette that is handed down to merchandising.

R.W.C.:   And then what are they handing over for you to work on?

Stringer: They hand me paintings that are done by artists. They hand me graphics that are created here in house, black and white or color. And all of this I interpret through the computer program and then recolor. I scan in the paintings, reduce them down to the final number of colors because it scans them in a large range (many colors), then I recolor them. We put them into production-ready repeats at this point so that what we're moving toward is actual technical communication with the vendors through modems. What we're going to be creating on the computer is actual to-the-millimeter print repeats that we can send to them (the vendors) and they just send them straight to the engravers. We also do all the stripes both woven and printed.

R.W.C.:   How much of the final fabrication is done on the computer?

Stringer: I'd say 90 percent of it now is done with the computers here which is great because you maintain a lot more control that way. If you're putting things into print-ready repeats here and no one is hav... having to reinterpret it anywhere else (at the mill), you don't lose the integrity of the design.

R.W.C.: Are all of the computers here connected to each other so you can share information?

Stringer: We've just started installing a network. We're going to communicate not only between departments but between companies. Everything's going to be networked together and everyone's going to talk to each other. And so that's going to really open up the way that we can use the machines because we'll be able to transfer information electronically back and forth. There will be a lot of benefits to that—production benefits and creative benefits. We really take the stance here of (being) a creative program. We're interested in the whole movement of forward communication and telecommunication, you know, modeming all of our files to vendors. Vendor communication is very important to us. It's a large percentage of what we spend all our research on right now. But we have to keep in mind that our processes are creative. We don't want to limit our creativity by being so focused on production. So there's a fine line that we have to walk. We really want to maintain the integrity—to maintain the control of our product, to lessen the cost, and create time savings and money savings. But at the same time, if we're talking about limiting our creativity then we're losing something for the gain.

R.W.C.: What happens to your output, does it go directly into a presentation for merchandising?

Stringer: Yes, four times a year we present our design orientation to the merchandisers.

R.W.C.: So that's done on boards?

Stringer: Yes, all flat output.

R.W.C.: And do you work directly on assembling those boards?

Stringer: No, the designers do those themselves with samples, of course. The boards are done for meeting purposes. Then they (the designers and merchandisers) break down and discuss them.

R.W.C.: Do the designers use the CAD systems themselves?

Stringer: The designers see the benefits of the system but they're not having to sit down and actually learn the program and do it themselves. In a lot of companies, the person who is using the computer becomes an operator. It's a different situation for each company. At the Gap, certain people have been motivated to be designers and they worked with that goal in the back of their heads while they were working (on the CAD programs). So they took on more creative control while they were working and then moved into design. The Gap happens to be very forward minded so that they would be more open to that sort of movement, be it vertical or horizontal. They want the employee to be happy and if the employee shows the motivation then the reward is given.

R.W.C.: How competitive is the industry in terms of getting a job in the CAD area?

Stringer: To be honest with you, this industry is very competitive. It always has been. If you're talking about going to work for a design company, you really have to work hard to achieve notoriety within the company, to be promoted, to be recognized for your creative abilities. It's no different with the CAD area. CAD provides you with an interesting position because it is a demanded position. The Gap needs somebody who knows how to run the equipment. So, experience working with CAD equipment offers you the ability to get into working at a company, but then it's all up to you to make your requirements, your needs, and your desires known to the company. If you don't push for a creative aspect, they may never give it to you because everybody wants to be creative and they want every one of the designs leaving their office to be their creation. You really have to work. It's just like any other position in the creative industry, you have to work to make your creative aspects known, to make your abilities known. If you do that, then you can move in that direction. It's just a matter of motivation and personal desire.

R.W.C.:   Do you experience a good level of job satisfaction?

Stringer: I like it here, but of course I work for the Gap, which is a great corporation. As far as the industry's concerned, it's one of the best to work for. It's because of how Gap feels about its employees, the product, and how they work within the market. It's also different than other Seventh Avenue companies because it's vertical. We design and sell the product. And that really makes a big difference in the attitude of the company a lot of times. I like it here a lot.

PREPRODUCTION

Preproduction processes include all of the computer-aided activities that help propel the designer's sketch to production. *Technical design* is often the term used to identify the mechanical rendering of flats and the development of **specifications (spec) sheets**. Often, the first pattern and samplemaking or on-screen sample viewing are included as well.

Spec and costing systems are communication links between design and production. All information pertinent to a particular style is recorded on a variety of forms for use in the overall process. These systems are also referred to as **product data management (PDM)** systems. A designer, technical designer, or merchandiser (depending on the company) will create a spec drawing of each style in a group or line. It will include exact measurements of the finished garment along each seam line and at fit points along internal lines and curves. There will be a size-grading chart indicating the relationship at each point of measurement between the sample size and sizes up and down from the sample. The type of fabric will be recorded as well as available colors, style numbers, and season. Any trimmings such as lace, buttons, and thread type will also be included. Later, in production, the cost of fabric and sewing processes can be added to the file along with the number of the marker, cut paths, and so on.

The information on the original spec sheet is used in many different ways within the company and on many different business forms. The type of form used is determined by the job at hand. For example, the patternmaking department would require a sheet that has the spec measurements and a size-grade chart so they could produce all of the patterns. The cutting department would not need the measurements, but it would require the style number, fabric and color information, and cut numbers from the sales department. The same information about a particular style should be able to be shared by every computer terminal in each department (design, production, and shipping and receiving) for use in whatever way necessary. All the data are electronically stored and identified in the same way, by the same numbers, style names, and so forth, for ease in communication and processing. Some software programs even record the number of forms that go along with each particular style so that professionals all along the line of production have access to a complete information network. Figure 3–7 shows spec-sheet variations. Other systems offer thumbnail sketch libraries so that designers can view past seasons' styles easily. Both silhouette and textile designs can be archived for retrieval when needed.

Depending on the configuration within a company, some technical designers will work with a pattern design system (PDS) or a **pattern generation system (PGS)** to go from the spec drawing to the first pattern. Using stored blocks and block components in the systems, the designer can assemble and modify the pattern parts into the new design. Since all of the components have been printed out and tested for accuracy and fit, the patternmaking department can often develop the production pattern for the garment without producing a sample. If a sample is necessary, instructions can come from the PDS system to a single ply cutter.

Software designers are currently working on converting a 3-D image to a 2-D image, and ultimately, to a pattern. Thus far this process has yielded positive results when working with tightly fitted foundation garments and swimsuits which now can be draped on a dress form stored in the CAD system (see Figure 3–8). As discussed in the preceding chapter, the various weights and drape characteristics of individual fabrics vary so greatly that difficulties arise in creating the mathematical descriptions a computer would need to flatten the 3-D image into a 2-D pattern.

Technology is also available that allows for a pattern to be fit onto an inputted dress form or mannequin (see Figure 2–18). All of the preproduction technologies will evolve and in the meantime each design company or manufacturer will continue to develop its own processes based on the CAD systems it owns. The important element is that the systems designated for each phase of the process be connected to each other for greater productivity.

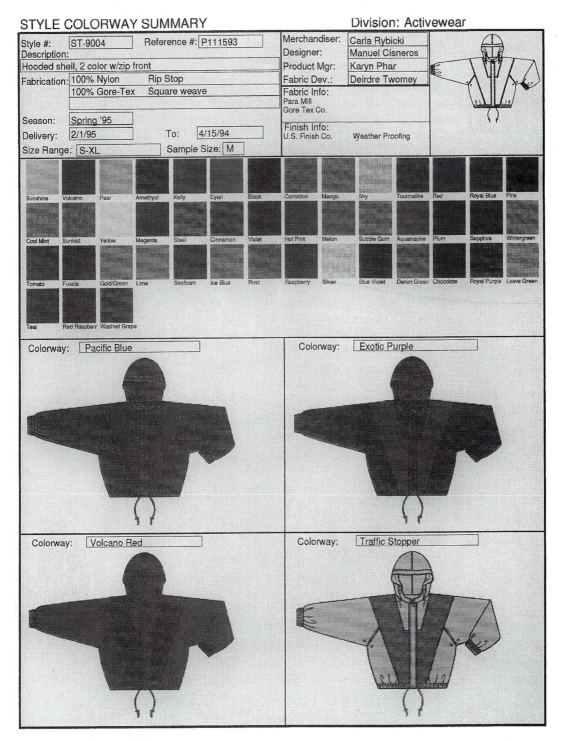

Figure 3–7   Three different spec sheets for the same garment (Courtesy of Animated Images, Inc.© 1995 Animated Images, Inc. All rights reserved.)

(*continued*)

STYLE COVERSHEET   Division: Activewear

Style #:	ST-9004	Reference #:	P111593	Team Manager:	Gerad Michaels
Description:				Merchandiser:	Carla Rybicki
Hooded shell, 2 color w/zip front				Designer:	Manuel Cisneros
Fabrication:	100% Nylon	Rip Stop		Product Mgr:	Karyn Phar
	100% Gore-Tex	Square weave		Patternmaker:	Todd Hanlon
				Prod. Engineer:	Chris Carone
Season:	Spring '95			Fabric Dev.:	Deirdre Twomey
Delivery:	2/1/95	To:	4/15/94	Sundry Dev.:	Christine Black
Size Range:	S-XL	Sample Size:	M	Testing Mgr:	Sharon Phillips

Final Style Approval: 8/ 1/94
By:

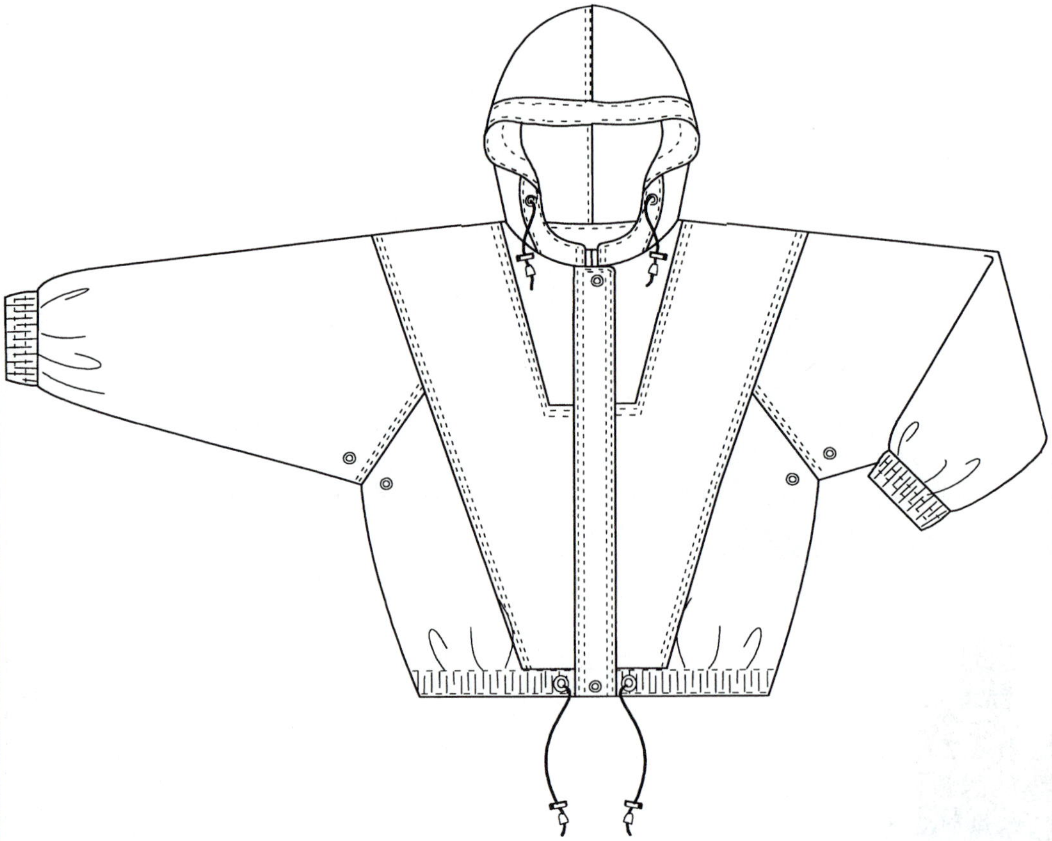

Figure 3–7 Continued

CONSTRUCTION DETAIL WORKSHEET   Division: Activewear

Style #: ST-9004 Reference #: P111593	Merchandiser: Carla Rybicki
Description: Hooded shell, 2 color w/zip front	Designer: Manuel Cisneros
Fabrication: 100% Nylon Rip Stop	Product Manager: Karyn Phar
100% Gore-Tex Square weave	Patternmaker: Todd Hanlon
Season: Spring '95	
Delivery: 2/1/95 To: 4/15/94	Production Engineer: Chris Carone
Size Range: S-XL Sample Size: M	

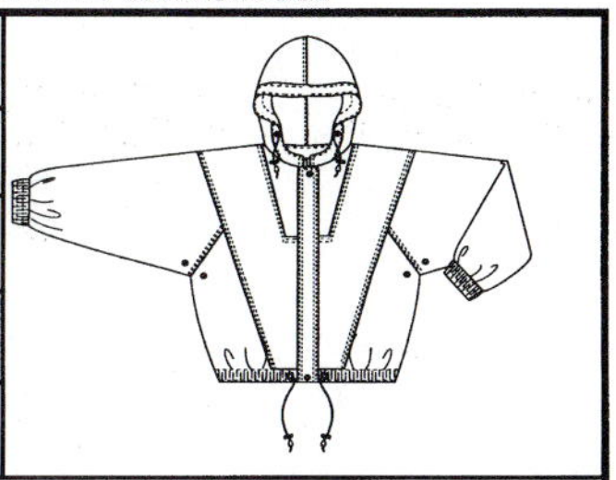

Design Comments:
Activewear shell for sport. Gromments underarm.

Construction Comments:		
Grommets one inch from underarm and armhole seams. Velcro strip behind placket one inch from top and bottom snaps.	Self Total 2.100 Contrast Total 0.850 Total Lining Total 0.230 Drawstring Total 2.450	Pattern ID#: ST2M4103 Spec/Sample ID#: STG41594 App'd Pattern Date: 4/14/94 Garment Weight: 8 oz.

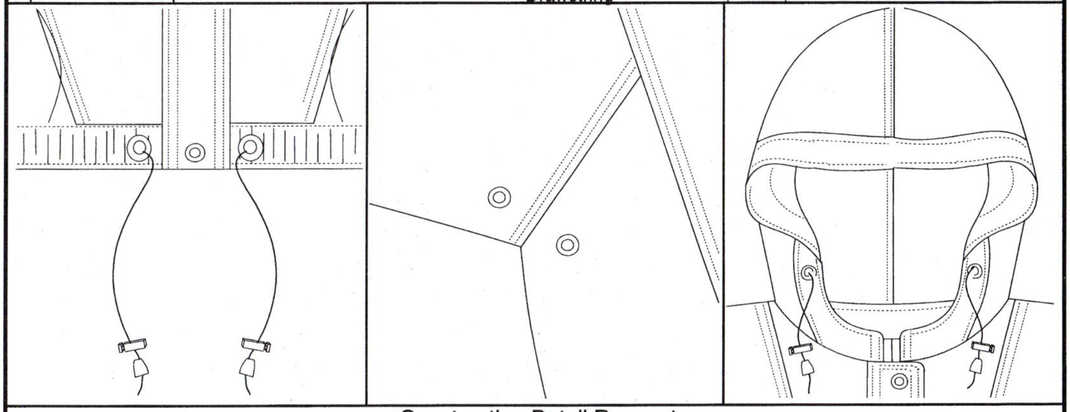

Construction Detail Request:

Part/Detail:	Description OR Dimensions:	Seam Type:	Lap?	Topstitch:	Bartack?	Fuse?	Press?	Fabric:
Waist	Casement	Clean Finish	---	-----	--	--	--	Self
Cuff-elastize	1 1/2" finished		---	3 Needle	--	--	--	Self
Contrast V	Pieced	Flat Fell	COS	2 Needle	--	--	--	Contrast
Placket				2 Needle	--	Y	--	Self
Hood	Casement				--	Y	--	Self
Drawstring	4 Ply-Cording							Trim
Hood Lining	Full Lining							Lining

Figure 3–7   Continued

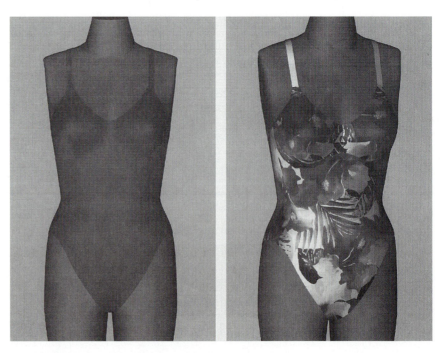

Figure 3-8 3-D draping simulation on a mannequin; Design Concept™ 3D System (courtesy of Computer Design, Inc.)

Photo credit: Laura Satori

Interview with William Forrester
Director of Computer Systems
Chaps, Ralph Lauren

Forrester: Originally, I was a chemistry major at the University of Florida—I was taking predental classes—I always wanted to be a dentist, so I was really into biochemistry and all that kind of stuff. Then one day I decided I had better reevaluate my creative side because I was getting bored. I had a technical mind and a background in mathematics, so I did a lot of thinking about how best I could uti-

lize my skills. Finally, I settled on textile production management, and I decided to go to the Fashion Institute of Technology
in New York to pursue a degree. I was probably the geekiest student there because between my right and left brain, I was getting
a bit closer to finding the place where I belong. On one hand I
had logic, but I also found the visual stimulation that I needed.
Of course, the field that I now work in incorporates not only computers but every aspect of the business as well.

R.W.C.:   How did you get started with this company?

Forrester: I started at Chaps, Ralph Lauren as an intern in the sweater division. They had a basic CAD system and I wanted to learn sweater
graphing and some of the more difficult aspects of technical
design on the computer. I was passionate about learning.
Basically, I was a sponge and absorbed as much knowledge about
the industry as I could. I guess my enthusiasm showed—the people at Chaps liked me, and I ended up freelancing for them for
about eight months. After my internship ended, Chaps offered me
the position of associate product manager, a title which they created especially for me. I worked in all areas of the business but
especially in knits and sweaters. Eventually I was given the task
of researching and buying a new CAD system, but I wanted something more than a basic design system. I wanted something that
could help manage all of the paperwork, etc.

R.W.C.:   So you were interested in building an information network as part
of your CAD system . . .

Forrester: Yes. After extensive research, I developed a comprehensive plan
to take the merchandise from the front end of the business—the
design, colors, fabric, and the garment—and put it all into a rela-
tional database. I chose a CAD system which would be easy to
operate—a multistation program called Primavision. At the same
time, I was rethinking the idea of form management. Why aren't
we on a network? Why aren't faxes sent via the computer? Why
aren't forms computerized? I found a company called Animated
Images that has a program called StyleManager© to help me deal
with all these questions. I think StyleManager© is going to save
my life.

R.W.C.:   How are you using the Primavision system now?

Forrester: On the CAD system, we do almost everything from scratch. Sweater
graphs, yarn dyes—almost anything along those lines works
much better now because the CAD system allows us to better communicate our ideas than the old method; i.e., painting or doing a
minibody and then sending it to the factory. A designer has to be
able to communicate the line he or she is developing, we have to
show that line to prospective buyers, and we also have to show
management what we do as well.

R.W.C.:   So are the roles of designer and merchandiser really blending?

Forrester: Yes, I think so.

R.W.C.:   And how are you using the Animated Images system?

Forrester: Dealing with paperwork is probably a designer's headache. And as a result of all the paperwork, most menswear designers don't spend enough time designing. A designer should be able to focus his or her energy on technical design, detail, trends, buttons, and the like instead of on pushing paper. I took these ideas (details, buttons, etc.) and built a database around them—a library of sorts. StyleManager© takes the work from the CAD system and directs it to the different places it needs to go—into a line list, a body, a spec sheet. The information lives in one place but filters out to different areas. I wanted to develop something that would follow the product from beginning to end, so that I could incorporate everything from merchandising to developing retail analyses and planning merchandise. Basically all of the information involving a garment from its development to its sale is contained within a loop. Using this program will allow us to create a better and more efficient business by analyzing what we are selling *and* what the customer wants.

R.W.C.:   Have there been obstacles to putting this computer system into place?

Forrester: Changing people's mindsets has been difficult—getting them to realize it's time to jump on the technological bandwagon. Companies like Chaps are growing so fast that if they don't grab hold of technology like a CAD system, well, it's like a snowball effect—soon they'll be left in the dust. I feel that we jumped on at exactly the right time—at a good point for our business. I want to integrate information, make it comprehensive, and make our buyers go "Wow."

R.W.C.:   How about the savings in costs to the company since you brought the CAD system in?

Forrester: We have made our biggest savings by reducing the number of color copies and the use of painting services. In less than two years, we will have saved more than enough to cover the initial investment—and the savings will continue. Eventually we'll be able to cut back on all our samples because we'll be using CAD simulation of the fabrics. Our salespeople will have a more visual and accurate representation of the line. Buyers know our company, so they don't necessarily need to see samples. Buying has changed dramatically in the last few years. It's a completely new ball game. Now it's all a number game. It used to be "Oh, I love that pattern," but now it's all about demographics—it's all based on information. So if we can apply and manipulate the information at the design end of the process, the buyers, in return, will buy the whole store concept, the floor layouts, everything. So you're not only saving money for your company, you are also making money.

R.W.C.:   Are buyers comfortable placing an order from computer output rather than real samples?

Forrester: We still use real samples, but the salespeople are now using the computerized version and, yes, [buyers] are completely comfortable with it.

R.W.C.: What was the reaction of the sales staff like?

Forrester: They love it! The computer output has made their lives so much easier. It's easier to see groups of items all on a page at once, it's better to evaluate the different styles. Our salespeople are crazy about it and so is the president of our company and just about everyone else.

R.W.C.: Do you foresee a time when salespeople could communicate with buyers by computer?

Forrester: Yes, definitely. I'll be at home . . .

R.W.C.: On the beach, with your laptop. How long have you worked for Chaps?

Forrester: Almost two years. I feel that I have accomplished what I set out to do, and now I'm at the final leg of my journey at Chaps. The opportunities are tremendous at this point—it's not too late for companies to take the plunge. I never had any formal training in computers, but I was able to take a concept and run with it. Basically I taught myself whatever I needed to know.

R.W.C.: In terms of menswear specifically, what makes using the computer so helpful?

Forrester: The business is based on numbers—it all comes down to the bottom line. If a silhouette works, for example, then we'll keep it in the line for the next three years. We process that information and run it over and over again just by changing the patterns. If you have a plaid in your computer and merely redo the color situation, it can look like five completely different plaids.

R.W.C.: How do you manage to keep up with technology in this field?

Forrester: You can't really stop long enough to get caught up, but, on the other hand, if you don't catch up, how can you get ahead? I've worked many, many weekends to bring the CAD system in. Once it was in, I began streamlining all of the departments. What I want people to know is that they should jump on the bandwagon, take the plunge. I have learned unbelievable things, and although I want to go back to school to become a computer geek, I think I'll wait awhile. There's still too much to do, too many fires to put out.

PRODUCTION

Many of the systems used in production have been discussed in the previous chapter because CAD began in these areas. Patternmaking, grading, marking, and cutting systems led the way for the development of illustration and preproduction systems.

Patternmakers have many more options now for producing patterns than they did in the early years of CAD. In the past, a hard paper pattern had to be digitized as a way of recording its dimensions in the computer. Now there are pattern scanners that reduce the time required to feed information about an existing pattern into the computer (see Figure 2–12). Pattern shapes can now be traced using a pressure-sensitive table and the image appears on screen. Using this system, a patternmaker can make adjustments to the pattern on the table with traditional tools such as a ruler and hip curve. All adjustments will appear on the display monitor.

As a company's library of patterns increases with each successive season, blocks can be reused and new patterns can be generated on screen through modifications that employ drawing tools or word command. The more the patternmaker reuses and modifies existing and tested patterns, the fewer samples have to be produced and the greater the savings in costs.

Once the patternmaker has saved all of the pattern parts for a particular style, the pattern goes from the PDS or PGS system to a grading system and then to a markermaking system. In these systems, the original pattern is seen on the screen in miniature and the grading function will show each newly generated size in a different color. The grade rules, or the way the pattern shrinks or grows at predesignated points within or along the perimeter of the pattern piece, are established individually by each company and applied to a certain garment. Grade rules can vary from style to style depending on the desired fit and proportion of the garment. The sized sets of patterns produced by the grading function are all **nested** inside one another so the patternmaker can check them for accuracy (see Figure 2–13).

The markermaking function now takes over and all the pattern pieces for each particular size are placed between two lines on the screen that represent fabric width. The computer will squeeze the patterns together as economically as possible and provide the operator with a calculation of fabric waste for that particular marker. This process represents an enormous dollar savings to every manufacturer who uses a markermaking system. If fabric for a particular style costs ten cents per inch and a markermaking system can save just one inch per garment, there is a savings of $100 when cutting a lot of only 1,000 pieces! Once the marker is completed, the exact cost of the fabric used for each garment can be calculated and used later to determine the final wholesale cost of the garment.

Plan cutting is established based on the real and projected orders for a style by size and color. The total number of pieces needed by size and color is fed into the markermaking system and the **lay plan** is created. This is the number of layers (plies) of material in each color that have to be stacked by the **cloth spreader** to satisfy the orders. The result is a cut ticket, or instructions to the cloth spreader and cutter, that specifies the appropriate number of fabric plies to be stacked. Some systems provide cut path instructions that tell the automated cutting machine which path to follow for speed and accuracy in cutting the fabric.

When actual costing for the final garment is completed, yardage figures from the markermaking system are used. Production departments also have computerized costing and production sequence planning options in their systems so the exact piecework operation sequence can be established and priced out. This all connects with the preproduction paperwork mentioned previously, and the costs for trims, thread, findings, packaging materials, and so forth are all added in to establish the final price of the garment.

Assembly processes include bar coding each piece of fabric so that all of the parts to a garment are matched together. A new technology that is currently being introduced to identify garment parts is **radio frequency tagging**. This process will use tags embedded in the garment parts which will only be readable by computers.[13]

Assembly line systems are available in which workstations throughout the factory are connected via overhead pulleys. **Garment-moving technology** lets garment parts be clipped onto the line and moved from station to station through the production plant (see Figure 2–19). An operator at a station will pull the work down, complete the appropriate machine function, and let the piece move on to the next station. Sewing machines are also computerized in many different ways so that high-quality work can be produced more easily and with great accuracy.

Robotics is an area that has been difficult to integrate in the soft goods assembly process. Since fabric thickness and texture vary so greatly, it is difficult for a machine to make the tactile adjustment. However, this technology is being worked on continually and will be integrated more and more into the large factory setting.

Photo credit: Laura Satori

Interview with Donald Savalli and Johnny Sample
Markermaking and Grading Specialists
Jones New York

R.W.C.:   What was the transition like for you in going from making markers by hand to doing your job on the computer?

Savalli: When we made markers by hand, the table must have been 25 to 30 yards long, maybe even longer. We used to have to lay those patterns in as tight as we could, and then after we got the patterns the way we wanted them, we had a machine that took a picture. Well, it didn't really take a picture, it was traced onto special (photosensitive) paper. It took a lot of time. Then we had to go and develop it ourselves and we had to record all the plot lines, strike lines, all that. When the computers came, I personally had a very hard time, because I could not understand that computer. To tell you the truth, I didn't like it. I wanted to pick it up and throw it out the door. It took me a long time to learn what I had to know to do my job. But now, that computer . . . you can't beat it. I mean, it's ten times faster, you don't have to be on your feet all day, you sit down and everything is on the little screen. It's a lot easier to make that marker looking at the whole thing than it is when you're out on the table and you can only see one little area at a time. Everything is up there in front of you, it's just so much easier.

R.W.C.:   Do you have any idea how much fabric you're saving?

Savalli: Yes! The computer tells you everything. It tells you what the length of the marker is, it tells you how much fabric you're utilizing, it tells you everything.

R.W.C.:   How many years have you been making markers and how many years have you been at Jones New York?

Savalli: I've been here 20 years, I've been in the business for about 31 or 32 years.

R.W.C.:   How long did it take you to be comfortable using the computer?

Savalli:	A long time . . . six to seven months. I really had a hard time because I don't really think I wanted to accept it. I wasn't comfortable. The little error messages kept appearing on the screen and I was frustrated . . . I mean, there was a time when I was just going to quit. It seemed that there was a lot of little things to remember just to do one little thing. After I got to understand it, it didn't seem that much of a big deal. Now, it's automatic. I mean, computers are the greatest thing that ever happened to me.
R.W.C.:	How about you, Mr. Sample. How long have you been working at Jones New York?
Sample:	I have been here three years and I've been working as a grader for 40 years. I worked at Albert Nipon right before coming here.
R.W.C.:	How did you adjust to grading patterns by computer?
Sample:	Converting from manual grading to computer grading wasn't very hard for me. But some people couldn't accept it because it's advancement, it (seemed to) hurt a lot of people. Where you needed five people before, with computers you only needed two. But I find that computerized grading, or marking or whatever, saved this industry thousands and thousands of dollars.
R.W.C.:	So when did you learn to use a computer?
Sample:	We were sent to Texas to learn the system, back in the 1970s. At that time, it was the Gerber/Camsco system and we spent two weeks there. In manual grading, we used to roll out the paper, mark up the paper, and mark up the sizes. It must have taken us two hours or more to do two or three sizes of a garment. In Texas, we were told that grading (the process) is the same but it would be set up in a different manner and names would be changed. The only big change was digitizing and we found out that we saved paper, we saved time, we saved aggravation. The computer itself builds up the pattern, the patterns are graded for you, and you check the grading of the nest. If the nest is OK, that's it. That eliminates cutting eight sets of patterns. It saves paper, time; you're home free.
Savalli:	As far as markermaking is concerned, if you make a fully lined jacket on a table, you would take all day. All day to just make one marker of that style. On the computer you could do three. You're tripling your productivity with that computer; it's a lot of time and money.
R.W.C.:	With all of this new technology that we have now, do you think that people still have to learn to make patterns and markers using traditional manual methods?
Sample:	Yes, you can't just come in and pick up the new stuff if you don't have the background.
R.W.C.:	So you couldn't take a pattern and learn how to grade on the computer alone?
Sample:	No. To me, if you don't start at the bottom and work your way up, then you lose a lot. Classrooms give you the basics, but once you get out of there, the only way to experience things is to get your

hands in it. You need to learn the basics in any field. Then technology can be applied and you learn from the people you've encountered, you gain experience.

R.W.C.: Do you feel the same way, Mr. Savalli?

Savalli: Sure. If you were a computer grader, or a computer markermaker, and the computer breaks, you're dead. But if you start from the bottom, when the computer breaks, you can still get a piece of paper, you can still grade. If you don't have that background, when that computer goes down, everything stops. A couple of days doing nothing can really hurt a company. Even without the computer, I can still go around that table and make a marker if I have to.

PROMOTION

Promotion of fashion is done on many levels. Designers promote their ideas to merchandisers and vice versa. Merchandisers present ideas to the sales force and the sales force promotes to retailers. The public then becomes part of the system through in-store promotions, direct mail, advertising, and all forms of media.

It is beyond the scope of this book to delve into video technology, television, and other forms of marketing and advertising in the apparel industry. We will concentrate on in-house functions, that is, communication among designers, merchandisers, salespeople, and retailers.

Textile design, illustration, and sketch programs are used by designers and merchandisers as vehicles for developing and editing new lines. Once the lines are developed, presentations are made to communicate the direction for a season. These presentations can be made by the designer to the merchandiser or to the sales and marketing staff, or by merchandisers alone to the sales and marketing staff. Sales personnel can then work with a retailer directly, or the designer and/or merchandiser can work with the retailer or customer who is interested in developing a private label program. Depending on the type and intent of the presentation, computers are used in various ways.

The purpose of the presentation board is to communicate color, fabrication, theme, and silhouette (see Plate 9). This will be discussed in more detail in Chapter 8. Often, flats are colored using all of the options for a seasonal palette and superimposed on each other to show the buyer or customer all the color choices. Colorways for prints, stripes, and plaids are communicated in presentation boards. The end result should show the viewer all of the possible choices in a group in a concise, easy-to-understand manner. Ultimately, a good line board will reduce the number of real samples that need to be made.

Although some industry-specific CAD programs do allow for assembly of various images into a single document for catalogue development, often textile designs and flats are imported into commercial software packages such as Quark XPress™, Adobe PageMaker®, and Adobe Illustrator® for their specific graphics capabilities. They are especially useful when catalogues and other printed mailers are required. Hang tags, logos, and labels of all kinds can be designed with this software and printed easily.

It is important to note the increasing importance of multimedia in the fashion arena. Many companies use CDs in their in-store or direct mail presentations to customers. CAD suppliers for the fashion industry have come up with software that aids a designer in creating a movie or on-screen fashion show based on the new designs for a season. By integrating various systems, such as textile design for the fabric and a sketch system for the silhouette, and then transferring the new garment to a model in a 3-D draping system, the clothes can be seen on models walking down a runway in a full-fledged fashion show, including music and/or commentary without a single sample ever having been made!

Photo credit: Laura Satori

Interview with Holly Henderson
Designer
Federated Product Development

R.W.C.:   How did you first become involved with computers?

Henderson: My background with CAD and computers started in the early 80s. I went to FIT and studied fashion design. I specialized in knitwear and I really loved creating my own fabrics. One of my first jobs in the industry was as a knit designer working for some factories in Brooklyn. I had to get samples done in a hurry and it was very frustrating in terms of working with the technicians because they never had time to do samples. They were always working on production. At that point, CAD didn't really exist. I became involved with computers out of pure frustration. I worked with a technician and he sat me down in front of his little Apple computer and told me to use keyboard commands and keyboard symbols to indicate the colors that I wanted in a jacquard pattern. So I used a star for a red color or an *A* for a blue or whatever I needed to do. I plugged in my little jacquard patterns which made the pattern tape to make my samples. And then as CAD developed, I became more and more interested in learning more about it. I worked on one of the very first CAD systems which was a Microdynamics system and I primarily used it for knitwear. At that point, we had about eight color capabilities—eight colors and I thought this was wonderful! I didn't have to look at everything in black and white anymore. I was really excited. I began doing presentation boards, sweater patterns, and sweater graphs that I would send over to the Orient. I could do full sweater fronts and prior to that time I would graph out my sweater fronts by hand and it took me a couple of days if it was an intricate pattern. Back when I was graphing by hand, if I wanted to change something, I'd have to start over from scratch. The company I was working for was going through some changes and I decided to start doing some freelance design work. I quit and went off on my own. Ironically, Macy's was one of my first clients, and here I am again.

R.W.C.:   Did you do freelance design using CAD systems?

Henderson: My husband and I came up with this idea—a design studio using CAD for the industry. So I started on my home PC computer and my husband and I worked out a little program that could just do little knit graphs on the computer. There wasn't anybody out there that was doing it back then, so we put our business plan together and in 1988 we opened the first real textile design studio for the apparel and textile industry. Although we specialized in knits, we did a little bit of everything. We used the Shima Seiki equipment which has very high-end graphics capabilities for manipulating and draping and photo-realistic imaging and texture mapping. We did a lot of that as well as print designs and recoloring prints. We had a whole staff of students that would do service bureau work and I had a client base of people that I would do design and merchandising presentations for.

R.W.C.:   What was it like back then? Did people accept computer output?

Henderson: It was extremely difficult. When we first started, we were very excited about the whole concept. We thought that everybody who saw this would think it was the greatest thing since sliced bread. But there were drawbacks and limitations. Designers were very reluctant to even come up to our studio to look at the equipment because at that time everybody thought these machines were going to take their jobs away—you just press a button and it's going to be done. Now they realize that's not the case, but at that point it was just lack of knowledge on their part. They didn't know what computers could do for them. At the beginning it was very, very difficult. So I took a full-time job with Federated which was one of my clients. They had CAD equipment that was really untapped for textile and fashion design.

R.W.C.: What system did they have?

Henderson: They were on Macintosh platforms and they were using the Monarch software and a variety of off-the-shelf things. At Federated, I was responsible for design and merchandising of sweaters, cut-and-sew knits, and active sportswear. I developed fabrics, prints, stripings, and jacquard patterns for sweaters using CAD and put together merchandising boards for meetings. Federated really never did that to the extent that I did. They were not really utilizing the full potential of the systems, so it was really a great opportunity for me.

R.W.C.: Were your clients able to understand and accept CAD work at this point in time?

Henderson: The buyers were very reluctant to look at a CAD printout at first. They had trouble understanding the CAD printout versus a painting, but after a while, their eyes seemed to change, their eyes opened maybe a little bit. Soon they thought it was great because they would ask, "Can we just have a little more red, or a little more pink? Add a little more of this or that." And minutes later I'd come back with another printout and they saw the benefits. So their eyes became accustomed to looking at a CAD printout rather than an actual painting. They thought it was great to see the actual print on the sketch and the whole thing put together. It gave them more of a flavor of how the whole line or the whole group would be put together in the stores. Beyond doing little lines and groups, we also did floor plan layouts so we could actually set up their departments in the stores. We actually set up their departments for them so they could send that information to their managers to know how to set up the floor.

R.W.C.: How long were you with Federated?

Henderson: Just about three years. And then recently we acquired Macy's and Macy's product development area was a lot more developed than Federated's product development at that point. So we (Federated) moved down here to become part of Macy's product development and I'm now working within the graphics and CAD design world here.

R.W.C.: Are you considered a designer or a merchandiser here at Macy's? How is the differentiation established?

Henderson: My title is designer, but designers have to be somewhat merchandisers and merchandisers have to have design backgrounds, and also be designers. It depends on who you're talking to and how they perceive a merchandiser. The designer's role is pretty clear cut: You have ideas and you execute the ideas and your goal is to get a final product or a final line. Merchandisers, in some people's eyes, are more or less numbers oriented. They plug in quantities of styles and price points rather than getting involved in how the pieces and the parts and the individual items go together. So, I guess I'm a designer and a merchandiser, except I don't get involved here with orders, or quantities, or setting prices. A merchandiser also has to follow up on production in many cases, and again it depends on the company, it depends on the job. For some companies, I was considered designer and merchandiser but I didn't get involved in the production. I would approve my final samples and approve production pre-samples or whatever, and that was the end of my responsibility. If there were production problems, of course I got involved. Some companies feel that merchandisers should see everything through until the product is landed in the stores. They also have to track in-store sales by style and color. So it could be very number intensive depending on the extent to which it's taken. Because Federated and Macy's have so many divisions now—Federated has eight different divisions and now with Macy's we're adding two more—trying to track all the merchandise is a monumental job.

R.W.C.:   It seems that sometimes merchandisers are hired to do the design work. Do you encounter this situation? Do you sense that it has repercussions?

Henderson: Well, I think that's a problem within our industry. It has become such a knock-off industry and merchandisers who consider themselves designers are really just going into stores, or shopping Europe, or pulling out magazine pictures and asking a designer to sketch it or come up with an idea, but "this is what I want it to look like." They are telling a designer what to do and not giving that designer a lot of creative freedom. I think that's where the designers get offended or feel that they're really not able to be creative.

R.W.C.:   I've seen that situation come up in the area of CAD where designers come to a company and they're hired as textile designers, and they end up recoloring.

Henderson: That's a high level of frustration. You have people that are very talented, they're very creative, they have had their education in textile design, and they end up recoloring or being a service bureau. That's what tends to happen, unfortunately. It's really the ignorance of the people that are giving them the projects that is the problem. If the people giving them the projects really understood what the equipment could do for them or really wanted to expand that capability, they could do it. A frustration I've heard from a lot of textile designers that are working on CAD is that they are just given these things that are simple, mundane kinds of things, and they're just executing things rather than designing.

R.W.C.:   They're CAD operators rather than designers . . .

Henderson: Exactly, and there's a difference. I think when you are first learning CAD, you need to be a CAD operator, you need to understand the mechanisms. When you're learning CAD, it's fine. But when you go beyond that and you really are a creative person, and not just a technical person, then that's where the frustration lies for real designers.

R.W.C.:   So where do you see it heading, say, ten years from now? As the industry is moving now, how will CAD unfold even more than it has?

Henderson: Well, I see CAD evolving in terms of technology, I think the technology will get sharper and faster. I also see more in terms of multimedia and CAD as one medium that a designer will use in combination with other things to present a total line or get a final product out. I see CAD being used to research fabrics on CD ROM rather than going through library books. I see it used to view fashion shows on your computer screen and to take video clips and put new product into them. My problem is that I have all these ideas and visions of how things could be, it's just getting the companies to get there. They're not there yet. Hopefully, down the road, they'll understand. I guess it's because no one really has demanded this from them. As more and more designers and people that are working with the CAD world demand more from the software developers and the hardware developers within the textile and apparel industry, things will improve.

R.W.C.:   Do you think we'll still have to maintain some of our old hand skills?

Henderson: Yes, definitely. I'm an artist, I have an art background, I've been painting since I was three years old. My first love is oil painting and I would love to have the time to go back and do that. CAD has been just another medium for me as an artist. Some things cannot be reproduced with CAD. It's another tool and using it depends on what your end product needs to be. I don't think CAD is the be all and end all. I haven't achieved certain things like brushstrokes and watercolor effects totally on a CAD system and I've been working on them for a long time. For mass production, I do believe that most of the work can be done through a CAD system. I guess it depends on what the end product is.

R.W.C.:   There's just so much technology that a designer has to be aware of: new tools, new information, greater expertise . . .

Henderson: Exactly, yes. And they still have to know the basics, they have to know the basic painting techniques and how they can be applied to CAD techniques. Technology is expanding. Now you have pressure-sensitive pens and graphics tablets and you can achieve more of an artistic hand on prints. I think that will even expand more and there will be more airbrush techniques. It's just a matter of being able to use skills the conventional way and then apply those skills to CAD.

R.W.C.:   Are you finding now, as opposed to when you had your studio, that you can really sell product totally by printout, you don't have to have a real sample?

Henderson: Yes.

R.W.C.:   So buyers are open to CAD and expect it. Are they satisfied doing their business this way?

Henderson: Not 100 percent yet. But it is getting there and yes, we have sold many groups and many items purely through CAD presentations. While I was in my own business, I went down to J.C. Penney and Sears and actually sold groups with the presentation boards. It does work. I think more and more buyers are accustomed and everyone is accustomed to buying things from catalogues. I think that with CAD technology, the draping software, and the simulation software, you can actually show a representative picture of a sample that doesn't exist yet and people will buy it from a catalogue. So there's no reason that they shouldn't buy it from a CAD printout if the quality is the same and it's extremely realistic looking. We've actually had clients that were catalogue people that have used CAD pieces in their catalogues. So the consumer doesn't know the difference and they've bought the product from a CAD printout whether they knew it or not. People that have been in the industry and who know what CAD output is, recognize the difference. The average consumer has no idea if the product is real or simulated. I think simulated products would allow companies to be a little more creative and take some risks; not be so safe and not do the same crew-neck tee-shirt over and over again because it's been successful. I think CAD gives designers the opportunity to try new things and to be more creative.

STUDY QUESTIONS AND PROBLEMS

1. Select a garment from your closet. Describe all of the computer-aided design functions that could have been used to produce that garment from start to finish.
2. What is the difference between a texture-mapped image and a 3-D image?
3. Report on a new technological development in the apparel industry. This development can be related to any phase of garment design and manufacture. Use *Bobbin Magazine* or *Apparel Industry Magazine*.
4. Interview an older person who learned to use a computer on the job. Describe the transition and the employee's response to the technology.

Chapter 4

Design in Context: Understanding the Marketplace

Before picking up a pencil or a stylus, a marker or a mouse, a designer approaches his or her work with an individual attitude and a particular frame of reference. This frame of reference is a foundation of knowledge based on cumulative professional experience blended with current information on trends in color, silhouette, and fabrication. It also includes a designer's personal point of view—a combination of aesthetics with a personal attitude toward the product. For example, Oscar de la Renta's approach is toward rich, luxurious clothes for a sophisticated woman. Calvin Klein's approach is spare, simplistic, and elegant. Liz Claiborne dresses a mainstream American woman comfortably and affordably.

Every designer has a specific creative attitude toward his or her work that is directed and defined by certain parameters, including a personal or company vision of the product. Sometimes these parameters are referred to as limitations. The following is a list of some of the more general limitations the designer is concerned with:

Customer identity
Competitive cost of final product
Manufacturing cost
Production capabilities
Season
Delivery date
Accessibility of materials

Primarily, the designer's role is to work within these parameters, or limitations, and to create apparel for a particular audience or customer. The goal is always the same: to sell product. Each company's success is ultimately measured by the seasonal sales figures. The designer's foremost responsibility, then, is to understand the identity of the consumer of the product—to know

the customer in order to design something that that customer will want to own. The more that is known about the customer, the greater the chances are of offering the product that will fit his or her perceived needs.

Consider the profile of a young American woman in her 20s who is beginning to establish her career. She works for a bank and her salary is $22,000 per year. She shares an apartment in a small Midwestern city and dresses conservatively for work. Now compare that profile with that of a 45-year-old interior designer who lives in a $275,000 townhouse in a major metropolitan area and makes commercial design presentations to prospective clients about three times each week. It goes without saying that these two women have very different needs when it comes to buying their clothing.

The junior market is often quite challenging to design for. The customer in that market is a teen who is looking for affordable, trendy clothes. It is important that he or she look "cool" and current, but it is most important that he or she dress in keeping with his or her particular social culture. This group is drawn toward heroes in the music, entertainment, and sports worlds. Anyone designing clothes for the junior or young men's market has to understand the mind set of this group, what they like to do, and what clothes mean to them. The more able a designer is to identify with the lifestyle of his or her customers, the easier it will be to design clothes for them.

Along with a clear profile of the customer, designers should understand as much about the **marketplace** as possible. In broad terms, the marketplace is where goods are bought and sold. There are many things designers need to buy, or know where to buy, in order to come up with a finished product. Designers should know how to **source** the marketplace: how to seek out and purchase (at the most competitive prices, of course) the materials and services necessary for the production, marketing, and merchandising of their products. In other words, designers have to know where to find and buy piece goods, trimmings, and findings. Each of these are separate markets that designers must be familiar with. They have to know which companies offer the best color and trend forecasting services at the best prices. They have to source the contractors that will cut and sew the product if necessary. Which service companies will offer them the best and fastest CAD work if they don't have their own systems?

Along with understanding the marketplace for goods and services, designers should be familiar with the sales process: where and how the final product is sold to the consumer. Who does the buying, what are they looking for, when will they be buying for a particular season, and how much are they willing to spend? Designers have to understand and accept the challenges that buyers face and be willing to work with them in a cooperative way.

It is obvious from this discussion that a designer has many questions to answer before the creative work begins. In a medium- to large-size company, the designer has a lot of assistance answering these questions. The marketing and merchandising teams are well aware of the marketplace for selling the product and they give the designer important feedback. There are usually design assistants whose responsibility is to shop the market and come back to the designer with reports on what is available in the marketplace and in the stores. Design is a cooperative process and teamwork and information sharing is imperative.

The designer will use all of this accumulated knowledge as a way to inform his or her work. Since design offers infinite possibilities and variety, all of the pieces of information that a designer gathers before beginning to work can be seen as a way to define and channel ideas. The information provides limitations that a designer can use as springboards for creativity. He or she can be challenged by the notion of working creatively within the confines or parameters of the marketplace and the particular customer that the company is trying to reach.

WHO IS THE CUSTOMER?

The study of the customer is a science and involves professionals who are devoted to studying economics, sociology, and psychology and their impact on consumerism. Obviously, a designer cannot be an expert in marketing and consumerism, but the vast and highly technical research that is consistently being done in these areas is an absolute asset to the designer's knowledge base.

Making and selling clothing successfully is contingent on understanding and satisfying the needs of a **target customer**. Sophisticated marketing studies help create a clear picture of the general population, all of whom are clothing consumers. The initial considerations are: How many people are out there buying clothes? Where do they live? How much money are they earning? What kind of households do they live in? What are their levels of education? The answers to these and similar questions are relatively objective and are referred to as **demographic** and **geographic** studies.

Other influential studies involve **psychographic** and **behavioristic** questions which have to do with subjective issues: How much of the consumers' earnings are they willing or able to spend on clothing and what are they interested in buying? What kind of clothing do they wear for work? How do they spend their leisure time and what do they want to wear during their nonworking hours? Who do they admire? What kind of music do they listen to? What do they value? What are their priorities? Figure 4–1 offers some perspective on segmentation variables.

Marketing experts divide the general population down into smaller and smaller subgroups based on statistical likenesses in their profiles. For example, the population can first be divided by sex and then subgroups of females can be divided based on age. Subsequently, income and occupation can be analyzed. The

Major Segmentation Variables for Consumer Markets

VARIABLE	TYPICAL BREAKDOWNS

Geographic

Region	Pacific, Mountain, West North Central, West South Central, East Central, East South Central, South Atlantic, Middle Atlantic, New England
City Size	Under 5,000; 5,000-20,000; 20,000-50,000; 50,000-100,000; 100,000-250,000; 250,000-500,000; 500,000-1,000,000; 1,000,000-4,000,000; 4,000,000 or over
Density	Urban, suburban, rural
Climate	Northern, southern

Demographic

Age	Under 6, 6-11, 12-19, 20-34, 35-49, 50-64, 65+
Sex	Male, female
Family Size	1-2, 3-4, 5+
Family Life Cycle	Young, single; young married, no children; young married, young children under 6; young married, youngest child 6 or over; older, married, with children; older, married, no children under 18; older, single
Income	Under $10,000; $10,000-15,000; $15,000-20,000; $20,000-30,000; $30,000-50,000; $50,000 and over
Occupation	Professional and technical; managers, officials, and proprietors; clerical, sales; craftsmen, foremen; operatives; farmers; retired; students; homemakers; unemployed
Education	Grade school or less, some high school, high school graduate, some college, college graduate, upper level degrees
Religion	Catholic, Protestant, Jewish, other
Race	White, African-American, Asian, Hispanic
Nationality	American, British, French, German, Scandinavian, Italian, Latin American, Middle Eastern, Japanese

Psychographic

Social Class	Lower lowers, upper lower, working class, middle class, upper middle class, lower uppers, upper uppers
Life Style	Achievers, believers, strivers
Personality	Compulsive, gregarious, authoritarian, ambitious

Behavioristic

Purchase Occasion	Regular occasion, special occasion
Benefits Sought	Quality, service, economy
User Status	Nonuser, ex-user, potential user, first-time user, regular user
Usage Rate	Light user, medium user, heavy user
Loyalty Status	None, medium, strong, absolute
Readiness Stage	Unaware, aware, informed, interested, desirous, intending to buy
Attitude Toward Product	Enthusiastic, positive, indifferent, negative, hostile

Figure 4–1 Major segmentation variables for consumer markets (Adapted from *Principles of Marketing* by Philip Kotler, Gary Armstrong, and Richard Starr, Jr., Prentice Hall, Inc., 1993)

groups are subdivided again and again until issues such as label consciousness and loyalty, along with level of interest in trendy or high fashion looks, are considered. Ultimately, the goal is to pinpoint the segment of the market that the product will be targeted toward. This subgroup is referred to as the **target market**. The needs of the members of that target market have to be interpreted based on the statistical studies done by the marketing experts. Then, strategies for reaching that market are established by experts in the field and can be extended to include advertising agencies. This is referred to as **market positioning**.

Returning to the examples of the two women described earlier in this chapter, the young woman who works at the bank is part of a certain target market that is looking for inexpensive, career clothes that make her feel professional and attractive. The interior designer is part of a target market of well-established professionals who work in a creative industry and want to be seen as possessing style and individuality. When the designer clearly understands the customer in a particular target market, then he or she can try to hone in on offering that particular customer what he or she might be interested in buying. Designers' creativity and vision are extremely important when it comes to putting themselves into the mind set of the target customer.

Once the target customer has been "captured"—that is, they have bought a company's product—the company's marketing and merchandising teams can keep track of what particular styles and fabrications their customers have chosen. Color preferences can be tracked and all of this information can be used to further define their profiles. Computers are an invaluable part of this entire process. The impact of computer technology on retailing has been heightened with the current trend toward **database marketing**.

Database marketing is sometimes referred to as relationship marketing and allows the retailer to track the products customers are buying in order to customize their marketing strategies toward people with similar buying preferences. Databases can be shared or sold among retailers to make the process of zeroing in on the target customer easier. "Results are proving to retailers that purchase behavior is a much more reliable pattern of future buying patterns than basic demographics."[14] Ultimately, designers, through whatever scientific and creative means available to them, have to try to anticipate what the customer will need or want in the future—a formidable challenge for even the most accomplished designers and manufacturers.

LOOKING AT THE MARKETPLACE

The marketplace is where goods are bought and sold. It is not necessarily a physical location because so many present-day transactions are accomplished by catalogue and by electronic exchange.

Three major divisions are found in the fashion marketplace: primary, secondary, and retail. Each division has it own trade organizations, shows, and publications.

The **primary market** consists of the producers of the raw materials used in manufacturing clothing. This includes the fiber and yarns used to produce textiles as well as the textiles themselves and the findings and trimmings that enhance the product: linings, interfacings, buttons, zippers, and so on. Each of these is a subcategory and constitutes an individual and distinct market. For example, the textile market is one of a number of markets that a clothing designer has to be familiar with. The textile market includes a huge variety of mills, converters, and jobbers that produce woven and knitted piece goods.

A designer, along with an assistant or team of assistants, will shop the market to learn which companies can provide the fabrics appropriate for his or her product. He or she has to know which mills offer knits suitable in quality and price for a product for the target customer. The designer has to know which print houses to turn to for goods in their customers' price range. Sourcing the market for fabrics, findings, and trimmings is an important function. It means knowing what is new in the marketplace and where to find it as well as knowing where to go to find the **staples**, the goods and materials used season after season that make up the "meat and potatoes" of a line.

It is almost always incumbent on the designer or a member of the design team to find the right product at the right price. At the outset, the designer will know how much he or she can spend per yard on fabric. A price range will have been established based on the price point of the company's product line. If a company is making dresses that wholesale for $70 to $85, the designer can't use $40-per-yard silks imported from Italy. So he or she must know which mills to shop for fabrics in the $4- to $5-per-yard range. The same is true of the trims and findings. A mother-of-pearl button is lovely on a $1,700 designer jacket, but plastic is the choice for a $35 blouse.

The **secondary market** consists of those companies that use the products from the primary market to produce the finished merchandise. The designer and manufacturer are part of this market and they have to be familiar with what their counterparts are doing in their shared marketplace. This is known as "shopping the competition." Designers should always be analyzing their markets to see what other companies comparable to theirs are producing and the price at which they are offering their products.

The **retail market** consists of those individuals or companies that sell the finished product to the consumer. Buyers from department and specialty stores, chains, and discount houses are all part of this market. Sometimes they buy for one store and sometimes they buy for chains and groups of stores owned by a parent company. They, too, are armed with a great amount of information about the market segment that their particular store tries to reach and what their market will bear in terms of price and styling.

Retailers are well aware of trends and subscribe to forecasting services for fashion prediction.

Each store divides the buying responsibilities into segments and gives a particular buyer the responsibility to buy for one or more of them (see Figure 4–2). For example, men's, women's, children's,

Common Buying Categories

Womenswear

Sportswear and Separates

Active Sport Dresses

Intimate Apparel

After Five/Eveningwear

Suits and Coats

Blouses

Sweaters

Swimwear

Bridal

Furs

Maternity

Accessories

Shoes

Menswear

Suits

Formal Wear

Sportcoats

Pants

Coats

Sportswear

Active Sport

Shoes

Furnishings

Ties

Underwear

Sleepwear/Robes

Accessories

Shirts

Pricing Categories

Couture

Designer

Bridge

Contemporary

Better

Moderate

Budget

Figure 4–2 Common buying categories for apparel

and home furnishings may be the initial subdivisions. Then in the women's category there are coats, suits, dresses, sportswear, and so on. Each category is then broken down by price and even by function. For example, women's sportswear will go from budget prices to moderate to bridge to designer. A store then can offer the customer a jacket at $60, $120, $270, and $1,500. A store could also offer a jacket to the bridge customer that she might wear to work and then another that she would wear for more casual functions. In each category and subdivision, a company has to offer its market segment appropriate price, appropriate styling, and appropriate fabrication for her lifestyle.

All of this is to say that a manufacturer has to fill a specific niche for the retailer and should become a relied-on resource for its particular merchandise. The retail store will divide its selling space into separate areas for each category and subcategory. One manufacturer's product is likely to be merchandised in the same area of the store as a similar product from another manufacturer. The two manufacturers then become competitors since they are trying to sell to the same customer. Again, the designer has to be familiar with the competition—who they are and what they are producing—so a competitive edge can be maintained whenever possible. Design can become a very secretive process: There can be no "leaks" to the competition because those sales figures could hang in the balance.

WHERE DOES CAD FIT IN?

Computers are an essential tool at each market level. Although an overview of the types of available systems and their uses has been offered in Chapters 2 and 3, it is helpful to reiterate in the context of the marketplace.

In the primary market, computers are used to design yarns and weaves for the yarns. Often, they interface with the looms to produce fabrics. Separate systems operate for dobby weaves as well as jacquards. Prints, too, are designed using CAD systems and some systems go directly to digital printing thereby bypassing the engraving process. This is still a rather new technology and most print houses continue to work with screens and engravings. Knits are also designed on the computer and specific CAD systems drive knitting machines. CAD is certainly not new to the primary marketplace. It is here that computers got their start in the form of punch cards for the Jacquard loom more than a century ago.

CAD has made its most recent impact in the secondary market. Most medium to large companies use CAD systems in some form. Presently the greatest use is in the area of grading and markermaking, but this is quickly changing. Many companies have systems for preproduction and production process management as well as for textile design. CAD output is becoming an established method for presentations. Those companies that cannot afford their own systems hire the services of a CAD bureau or a freelance designer who produces CAD output for various clients. CAD service bureaus supply the trade with graded patterns, markers, print services (colorways and companion prints created from existing artwork), and presentation boards. These functions will be discussed in greater detail in later chapters.

Design teams in the secondary market are beginning to do their sourcing electronically. It is predicted that "**electronic sourcing** will become the standard method for finding contractors, suppliers, new products, and equipment by the year 2000."[15] The goal of industry leaders is to provide sourcing networks that would allow the designer access to information on fashion forecasting, competitors' products and strategies, and available textiles and findings. Images of fabrics, trimmings, labels, and so forth will be seen on the computer screen and orders will be processed immediately.[16]

In the retail market, a merchandiser will often sit at a designer's side in front of a CAD system. Together they can develop and refine new products for their stores by providing input from each of their particular vantage points. Aside from design, merchandisers use EDI (electronic data interchange) systems to keep track of sales and to communicate with the manufacturer. Because of this communication, the merchandiser can electronically advise the manufacturer when a reorder is needed. Problems with out-of-stock colors and sizes can be avoided and hopefully the customer will not leave the store empty handed because the size 6 pink jeans have already been sold.

Private Label

Private label manufacture and sales have become a sizable portion of retail sales. In the private label sector of the apparel industry, retailers create and produce merchandise under their own labels. These products are then sold solely from their own retail stores. The growth of the private label industry since 1990 has resulted in figures that indicate that in certain clothing categories—specifically, men's sport, polo, and work shirts, and women's blouses, shirts, and vests—an average of only 17 percent more branded merchandise was sold than private label merchandise.[17] This trend is consistent with growth in almost all other clothing categories. Retailers feel that they are in close communication with their customers' needs by virtue of the fact that they deal with consumers daily on the selling floor. They feel they can fill gaps left by brand name suppliers and offer their customer a greater variety of choices. Private label manufacture can often provide merchandise more quickly and at a better price than a brand name supplier can, so retailers develop their own labels, hire their own product development teams, and have their items manufactured privately.

When a store creates its own private label program, it combines the secondary market with the retail market because it is producing the merchandise that it sells. Many customers, however, still demand nationally known brand names, so retailers combine branded merchandise with their own private label products when stocking their stores.

Market Integration

Sophisticated systems of information sharing among all three market areas is a very current thrust of the CAD industry. Information from the mill can be shared with information offered by the manufacturer and then given to the retailer, who in turn can relate back to the manufacturer. The designer can create a print for a shirt and send the image electronically to the mill. The designer can do a flat sketch of the garment and send it to the retail buyer for approval—electronically, of course. All the specifications from preproduction, production, and costing are kept in the file, and the information can be shared by many employees of the company wherever they are in the world. Large companies are creating *Intranets*, or electronic communications systems, among all locations and personnel associated with the organization.

This capacity to integrate all aspects of the market via the computer and CAD systems is very vital to the positive functioning of a company. Many CAD systems suppliers use the notion of **connectivity** as an important feature in the systems they sell. This ability for computers to connect all phases of design and manufacture has been the basis of Quick Response Technology and flexible and agile manufacturing discussed earlier, and promises to bring goods to the marketplace more quickly and at a better price than in the past.

Electronic Shopping

One of the newest technological advances in retailing is **electronic shopping,** which is the ability to look at and purchase product via cable television and/or telephone lines. Many large retailers are afraid *not* to buy into this trend because of the income potential. Forecasters predict a "$150 billion market for electronic retailing by 2004" and also by the same year, "a five percent share of total retail sales."[18] Other figures support the consumer trend toward shopping from their computer terminals: "37 percent of American households own a personal desktop or laptop computer. Some seven million multimedia-equipped PCs were sold to homes in 1994, and seven million users subscribe to an interactive service such as Prodigy, CompuServe, or America Online."[19]

Customers can shop for a wide variety of products, including clothing, by watching 24-hour home shopping channels on

PLATE 1 Textile print simulation (Courtesy of Sophis USA, Inc.)

PLATE 2 (a,b) Simulation of plaid design in two colorways (Courtesy of Cadtex Corporation)

PLATE 3 (a,b) Jacquard weave simulation in two colorways
(Courtesy of EAT, Inc., The DesignScope® Company)

(a) Original scanned image

(b) Image after color reduction and cleaning

PLATE 4

(c) resized motif in repeat (Textile design: Lauren Sphar)

(a) The motif has been recolored for the seasonal palette and layered over a dotted ground

(b) a second colorway

PLATE 5

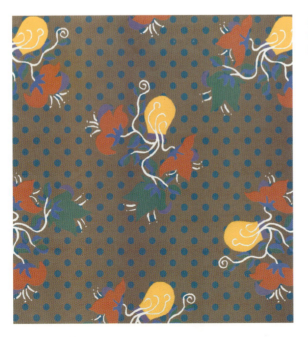

(c) a third colorway (Textile design: Lauren Sphar)

PLATE 6(a,b) A pair of companion prints in the same color story (Textile design: Lauren Sphar)

PLATE 7 Coordinated stripe (Textile design: Lauren Sphar)

PLATE 8 Coordinated plaid (Textile design: Lauren Sphar)

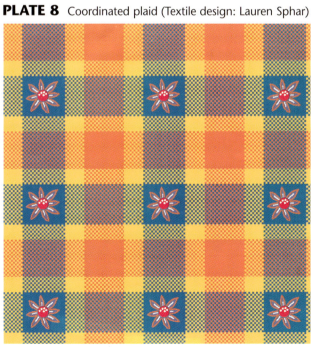

(a)

PLATE 9
A set of presentation
boards showing
(a) color and theme;
(b) fabrication; and
(c) silhouette
(Courtesy of
Jamie Durkin)

(b)

(c)

PLATE 10 Mood board for menswear showing South American influence, a neutral palette, and textural woven fabrics (Courtesy of the Wool Bureau, Inc. Service provided only to licensees of The Wool Bureau, Inc.)

PLATE 11 A romantic mood board for womenswear showing delicate, antique fabrics, faded pastels, and florals (Courtesy of The Wool Bureau, Inc. Service provided only to licensees of The Wool Bureau, Inc.)

PLATE 12 Munsell Color Tree
(Courtesy of X-Rite®, Inc.)

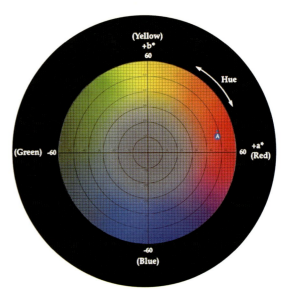

PLATE
CIELAB
color cha
(Courtes
of Minol
Corp.)

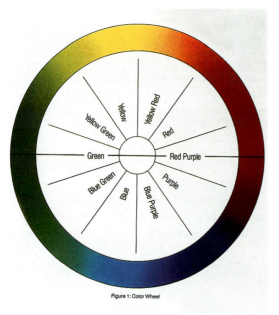

Figure 1: Color Wheel

PLATE 14 The color wheel
(Courtesy of X-Rite®, Inc.)

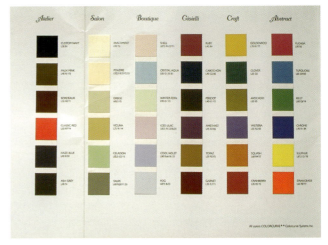

PLATE 15 Fall/winter color card
(Courtesy of Hoechst Celanese Corp. All colors
COLORCURVE® © Colorcurve Systems, Inc.)

PLATE 16
A seasonal palette
can be divided into
categories based on
color type or these
(Courtesy of The
Wool Bureau,
Inc. Service
provided only to
licensees of The
Wool Bureau, Inc.)

(a)

PLATE 17
(a-c) Samples of a
collection of textile
designs related to a
sun, moon, and
stars theme
(Design: Kathi
Martin Maddaloni)

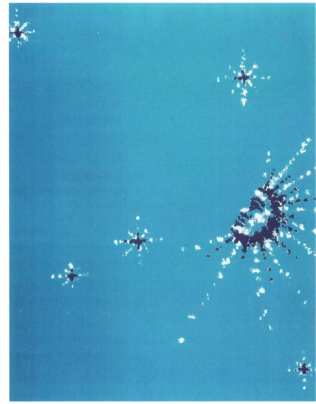

(b)

(c)

(a)

PLATE 18
(a-c) Coordinated
textile designs
based on an angel
and star motif
(Design: Kathi
Matin Maddaloni)

(b)

(c)

(a) Conversational cowboy print in a one-way
motif with a half drop

(b) two-way motif with a quarter drop

PLATE 19

(c) four-way motif in a tight arrangement

(d) open arrangement, tossed motif
(Design: Kathi Martin Maddaloni)

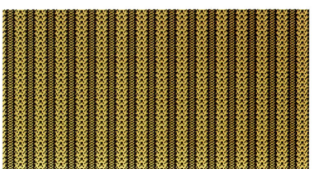

(a) Coordinated stripe motif created in the two-tone
custom pattern function in CorelDraw™

(b) second colorway of striped pattern
(Design: Kathi Martin Maddaloni)

PLATE 20

PLATE 21
"Square Spiral" originated in **Fractasketch** and put into
repeat in **Superpaint**, then into **JacWeave** by AVL
(Textile design courtesy of Jhane Barnes)

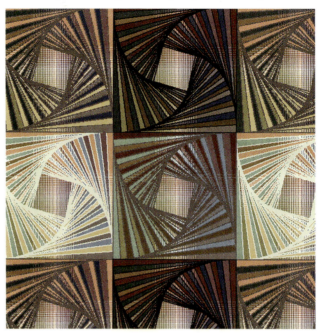

PLATE 22
"Castles" originated in the Vector Automata program
Expansions, put into repeat in **Color'in** by AVL. Weave
simulation in **JacWeave** by AVL (Textile design
courtesy of Jhane Barnes)

PLATE 23
Globalism and ethnicity are emphasized in this theme board (Courtesy of Jan Marshall)

PLATE 24
The focus of this trend board is toward geometry and shine coupled with western detailing (Courtesy of Jan Marshall)

PLATE 25
Nubby, tweedy, rugged, textural, and comfortable fabrics make up this fabric board for relaxed, weekend wear (Courtesy of Cotton, Inc.)

PLATE 26
This yarn board
shows a new type
of yarn in a range
of colors (Courtesy
of Jan Marshall)

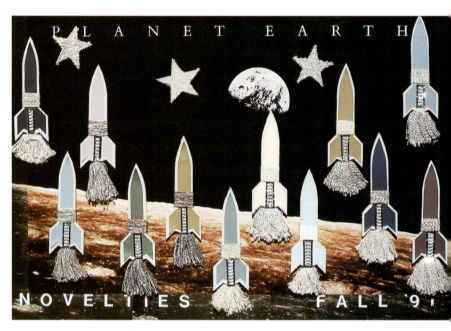

(a)

PLATE 27
(a,b) Computer-generated
line plan for Hartstrings
catalogue shows all of the
styles in a group (Courtesy
of Hartstrings, Inc.)

(b)

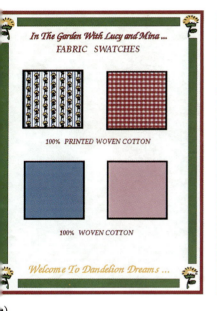

PLATE 28 (a-c) Computer-generated presentation triptych (Courtesy of Christian Kuo)

PLATE 29 (a,b) CAD generated presentation boards (Designed by Kenji Takabayashi)

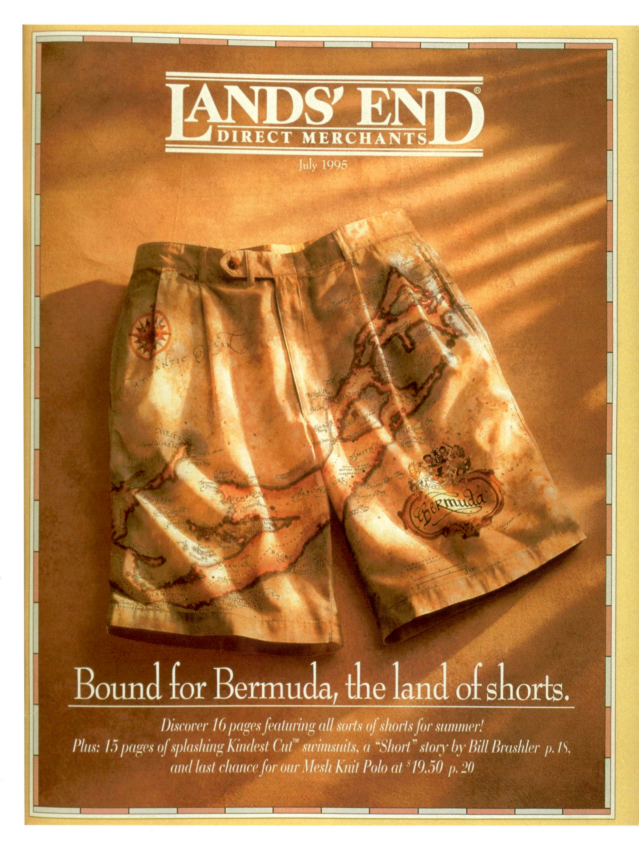

PLATE 30 Lands' End featured a virtual product on the cover of its July 1995 catalogue (Courtesy of Lands' End Direct merchants)

cable TV and then using their telephones to place orders. Stores including Neiman Marcus, Nordstrom's, Bloomingdale's, and Macy's have all sold products via television shopping shows. Youth markets enjoy shopping through MTV and the S shopping network.[20] "Infomercials," which offer much information about a single product as well as the opportunity to order it, are having much success, and the new direction in **digital interactive television** allows the shopper to communicate with the store by way of connecting cable lines with telephone lines for order entry. So the consumer can order an item from J.C. Penney or Nordstrom's that has been shown on television by way of the modem connected to his or her home computer.

CD-ROM catalogues are offered by many major companies and on-line shopping through the Internet and World Wide Web provide access to a "cybermarketplace" consisting of products from Spiegel, Sears, Land's End, K Mart, Wal-Mart, Marshall's, and many others. Many designers are retailers like GAP, Donna Karan, Armani, Versace, Reebok and Levi have established web sites in order to market their product. "Fashionangel" is a popular web site that offers fashion product information, company profiles, fashion magazines and more.

The technology is still in the very early stages and some are questioning how many shoppers will really buy soft goods without experiencing the tactile quality of the fabric and the fit of the garment. Other issues include how comfortable the average person is with all of the new technology, and security problems created by providing credit card information over the wires. Time spent on line downloading images is still very long. It seems, however, that the technology is here to stay and designers and merchandisers will be called upon to create and merchandise new products for the cybermarket if they plan on staying competitive.

A CONSUMER-DRIVEN MARKETPLACE

In recent years, the clothing industry has become more and more consumer driven. A great deal of energy and expense has been directed at understanding the consumer's needs and satisfying what these needs are perceived to be. As a result, companies are less prone to taking creative risks for fear that the consumer will not be ready or willing to try something new. This has led to too much homogeneous product in the stores and little excitement for the consumer; the overall situation has contributed to a soft retail market. The realization that the consumer may not know what they will want next season is challenging designers even further. So the designer must try to absorb all of the issues facing him or her and look to various sources of inspiration to stimulate his or her work.

Photo credit: Laura Satori

Interview with Haysun A. Hahn
Creative Marketing Director, Promostyl
Director of Color and Trends, Adidas International

Hahn: My responsibility as creative marketing director for Promostyl includes the marketing and handling of the company in the United States. I am also director of color and trends for Adidas International. I oversee both design teams and organize the colors for each new season. I dictate color combinations and which colors are important in each of the sectors. I also do some consulting for Samsung International in Korea. They are developing a streetwear line for kids and I oversee that. I also have a nonprofit organization for designers and arrange seminars twice a year. We get together somewhere in the world to talk about design ideas.

R.W.C.:   What is the function of a color service? Can you demystify how trends in color are established?

Hahn: The idea that color is just instinctual and disorganized is the mystery that we want to believe. This is because we have to leave room for creativity. But at the core, color helps to organize creativity. There is a kind of a campaign process that happens, so that the color message goes from one level to the next to the next . . . Half of our mission is to make sure that this progression actually happens. We research it (color), we look at the past few seasons and the way they have evolved and we have a very specific system for reading the color palette. We examine whether the emphasis is more toward green or more toward red. Is it shifting more from blues to greens or reds to purples? How influential is yellow to orange, so on and so forth.

R.W.C.:   Do you work with other forecasters to determine color direction?

Hahn: There are committees that decide on color within each separate company: Promostyl, Dominique Peclere, Nelli Rodi and others.

Each of those organizations will come out with its own color palette. But it isn't done in a competitive way. There is sharing, there are discussions. So for Summer 1997, for instance, we are going to talk a lot about turquoise to purple ranges. There will be variations of blues and variations of violets and this is going to be key.

R.W.C.:   How do you establish that direction? How do you know that it's going to go from turquoise to purple, for example? Is it based on sales from seasons before, or consumer choice?

Hahn: No, never! We look at the public as followers, not leaders. There is a very long period of time invested in seducing the public into following. We believe that if we are organized enough, the public will not have a choice by the time they go to the stores. We base it on the history of color evolution. We are physiologically limited as human animals in the way we absorb color. When it comes to color, we function according to a specific process. For example, if a grey/green is a trend, it will shift toward yellow which will bring us right back into blue. If red is a big color, we will know that this is not a color that lasts a long time, because it is a color that exhausts us. It just drains the energy right out of us. As does white. White is a very repellent type of color, so if we think about anything on white, it actually repels the color away from the white. That can be exhausting too. So you tend to resent those colors or to reject them very quickly. We are not an industry that wants to give the public choices. We want to make the choices for them. Within a very narrow span, we want to give them options, but not choices. We are not saying you can have chicken, fish, or red meat. We are telling them that this season it is chicken. Do you want it fried, or roasted, or baked? We just have one cycle after another after another. I would say 85 percent is absolutely scientific.

R.W.C.:   When you approach a palette for a new season, how do you make up the divisions among the colors and establish the different directions?

Hahn: You have to establish the divisions before you place color. If I talk about the season now, street influence has been a key issue. So I would organize the palette to have one impression of street, another impression of nature, and so on. The divisions get to be much more sociologically based than academically based. We do the trending and then we place the colors accordingly.

R.W.C.:   Is there always a nature segment, is there always a neutral segment? Are there certain established, definite divisions or themes?

Hahn: You know, it's absolutely cultural. In America we do have divisions. We always have a bright, pastel, neutral, and accent range of color. This is an American formula. In Europe, you see it organized in an entirely different way. They will talk about mid-tones, darks, and lights. In lights, there can be pastels as well as neutrals, as well as synthetic-based color. And then Asia does it their own way too. But there is consistency in terms of the overall direction rather than the divisions.

R.W.C.:	Do you advise either the designers that work with you or the companies that are part of your system how to use color ?
Hahn:	Sure, we have to. Because often it's not the colors themselves, but the way they are combined that is the issue. Take navy, for example. Navy was in this year's palette, as it was in last year's palette, as it was the year before. But, if we look at navy five years ago, we used navy, red, a little bit of gold, and off-white. We used it in a plaid with some nice green in it. Now, if we look at navy, we use it next to a neon-ish anise color. We juxtapose that with orange, and we put a burgundy next to it, and it has a totally different kind of life. Navy behaves like black did five years ago. We literally have to create menus, so color can be used in combination.
R.W.C.:	In talking about the evolution of navy from the early to mid 90s, what were the causes of the change?
Hahn:	We changed from the Republicans to the Democrats! With the Republicans, we wanted a slightly military, clean, cobalt-like blue—a conformist navy. But now that we have a Democratic president, who is younger, we have an economy that is picking up, we have more optimism. We have moderate everything—we have moderate conservative, we have moderate liberal, and this opens up the way we view traditional colors. So if you look at the color now, it looks more black. Culturally speaking, black makes us feel younger. There's always a reason why the shift happens. Even with red, orange, or yellow, it's often as simple as looking around you.
R.W.C.:	So you assimilate what is going on economically and culturally, and you translate that into color change. That change is coupled with the cycle that all color goes through in terms of movement from one hue to another.
Hahn:	Yes. If we say that colors are just like sounds, then you have to absorb the sound that is around you now. Then we can see how much of a difference in sound we can tolerate for the season we are working on. It's kind of like that. If we are looking at what's going on right now, we have to look at what is not obvious, we have to examine the sublevel. That is why we spend an exhaustive amount of time looking at alternative lifestyles, alternative music, alternative trends of any kind, because that's exactly what's going to pop up.
R.W.C.:	How does this information reach you? Do you have roaming scouts out there who are reporting new directions?
Hahn:	We have a staff whose average age is probably 19 or 20 and they are always looking at different things. Inevitably though, the final decisions are made by a staff that is probably in their 50s. They temper the input and make it digestible at other levels. Ultimately, it has to be meaningful to people in their 30s. I also think the other important issue in trending as a whole, and especially with issues of color, is that there are times in history when color means a lot. And there are times in history when color means very little. And the level of importance has to do with the

fact that we have emotional reactions to our perceptions of events in our culture. This has a very profound effect on the way we relate certain colors with certain moods. For example, we talked about navy. Navy is about tradition, about conformity. We have ranges of fuschia that are totally rebellious. We have other shades of purple that are very passionate. Right now we are experiencing an incredible amount of war, an incredible amount of generation gap, and we are seeing so much disparity and segmentation that we are feeling a little bit alienated and lost. So you have to always look at what the color means at a point in history. At the end of a century, where we are now, we are looking desperately for a way to connect. And we are going to do it with color.

R.W.C.: What span of time does it take for color to cycle?

Hahn: Even people who do trending will be very, very moderate in their opinions about how quickly people change from neutral to color. But it is a very huge jump, it happens very fast, and the people who dare, lead the market. People who are fearful literally have to wait another 15-year cycle.

R.W.C.: Are you saying it's a 15-year complete cycle as we move through color back to neutral?

Hahn: Yes, approximately. If you think about it, in the 70s, we embraced every possibility and every experimentation. And our fashions actually said that. We were discovering polyester, we were wearing dresses, heels, nylon-printed tight tee-shirts for men. We were experimenting and pushing everything that was possible to push. Now we are in the 90s, twenty years later, and we've got the energy back. By the end of the 90s we should start seeing conformist ideas specific to each group or tribe we belong to. It's very important to be specialized in something. It's not good enough to know a little about everything. You have to specialize. The unique thing that happened in the 90s, though, that has not happened in any other decade, was that for the first time we had a spiritual trend. There was an ecological, planet-conscience, cosmic thrust. But it didn't last. And you could bank on the baby boomer generation, who were as fickle and as easy to sway as we predicted: They dove right in and then moved right on.

R.W.C.: How did the spiritual trend translate into color?

Hahn: All of the colors that we thought should be recycled were important. Lots of people heard the word "eco," and they said they felt greens were very important, so the last few years have been about green. Green everything—even cars and furniture. Everything was naturalistically based. We used terracotta, lots of browns; we had black that looked brown, we blackened colors so they looked deeper and muddier. We appreciated grunge, we were into dirt.

R.W.C.: So what does this mean as we near the end of the century?

Hahn: Desperation! Everybody is desperate to be dramatic and to be different and to make a statement.

R.W.C.: How will that translate once we reach the year 2000?

Hahn:

I think whenever there is a turn of the century, we go through a retro phase in a very desperate way. As is typical with the pendulum, the farther it swings, the more extreme the swing becomes. So the more retro influence there is right now, the more advanced technology there will be to balance that. A good way of seeing that is through art. We have extremely experimental, bizarre, futuristic art forms now because technology as a medium affects creativity. Then you have the total opposite in that impressionistic paintings are very trendy right now. So, what does this mean? Well, there is great security, serenity, and comfort in impressionism because the other stuff is outright scary.

R.W.C.:

Let's talk a little about computers and your response to them. Color and computers and the difficulties with translating color are hot topics.

Hahn:

I think the limitations are not what we need to discuss anymore. I think what is important to focus on are the possibilities. I think if we talk about establishment designers in general, they will tell you limitations first. If you can get past the anxiety, there is nothing the computer can't do in the most effective way.

USING SOURCES OF INSPIRATION

It is obvious by now that the designer has to have an enormous amount of information stored in his or her mind before any actual design work begins. He or she needs to be armed with information about the customer, the marketplace, and the new technology. This knowledge is combined with creativity, intuition, and a great deal of common sense. Thankfully, most designers work as part of a team, with assistants, merchandisers, and retailers who help to direct their work and inform their decisions.

Design parameters are set by understanding the target customer and studying the market that supplies the materials and means to produce and sell the product. Then, design direction can be established. Designers are asked repeatedly: How do you come up with new ideas for your line? What happens if your creativity runs dry? Where does inspiration come from?

Inspiration comes from everywhere, from our environment, which is made up of the worlds of art, entertainment, politics, economics, technology, and on and on. If designers are receptive and "tuned in," they will find that they are being constantly barraged by sources of inspiration. They have to sort through these resources and carefully choose what has current value for their work. Timing is everything. This process may feel like a shot in the dark sometimes, but there are services and periodicals, newspapers and trade publications whose function is to inform designers about upcoming trends in their segment of the industry.

Designers must constantly pore over magazines, both old and new, and read trade publications and consumer reports.

Forecasting services research the market at every level: trend, color, silhouette, fabrication. They learn what people are wearing on the streets of Paris, Tokyo, and the Riviera. They know which movies, plays, and music will have an effect on culture. They make educated projections about what people will want to wear one or two years down the road. They are a vital part of a designer's livelihood. In a business as volatile and changeable as fashion, the designer has to be hungry for all types of visual and sensory stimulation and all of this is absorbed and translated into a vision of what is current and what the consumer might be interested in wearing.

Designers make a habit of keeping a sketchbook with them at all times to record any thoughts or images that are important. A designer will also keep many *clip files*: one for skirts, sweaters, textures, color combinations, details, and so on. These can be file folders or envelopes labeled by category. Whenever the designer sees something interesting in a magazine, he or she will cut it out and file it. Fabric swatches, travel brochures, and greeting cards all provide contents for the clip files.

More often than not, the direction for a season is determined by the design team in concert with the merchandisers. Sales information gleaned from past performance, current color and styling information from myriad sources, and predictions of what will be "hot" for the future season all combine to get the design process started. It is up to the design and merchandising team to assimilate all of this and put it into their own company's perspective, to develop a point of view for the season for their company. That point of view or mood is then pictorialized so it can be communicated to anyone in the company concerned with the direction of the line.

This pictorial representation can come in the form of a simple photograph, tearsheets from magazines (swipes), greeting cards, reprints from fine arts, or pieces of ethnic fabrics. These representations are the basis for establishing mood boards or concept boards which portray the feeling that the upcoming line will contain. A good mood board will be translatable by any number of people on the design team. The image is a representation of the inspiration and therefore inspires the development of the clothing.

The mood board often contains the color direction for the upcoming season and may offer some indication about texture and fabrication. The images in Plates 10 and 11 are examples of mood boards. Each one portrays a different attitude that can inspire design for a line of apparel. It is helpful to stop and examine the feeling induced by each of the images.

After the overall concept or mood is decided on for a season, a designer might want to subdivide the clothing category and create individual themes for each division. For example, a menswear company might select a powerful, athletic concept for a moderately priced sportswear line. Themes related to the overall mood could include a nautical feeling or a country club look. Each of these would be pictorialized in a theme board. These and other types of presentation boards will be discussed in the upcoming chapters.

STUDY QUESTIONS AND PROBLEMS

1. Create a customer profile of an imaginary person. What does he/she look like? Answer questions about occupation, workplace, marital status, and income. How many people live in the customer's household? Describe everything you can think of about your customer's tastes, habits, and so on.

2. Collect four photographs of people from magazines you have at home: a woman in her 30s or 40s, a teenager, a man in his 20s, and a child. Select one of them and save the other images for exercises in later chapters. Answer all of the questions raised in the previous exercise, but add favorite designers, brands, and colors. How much money does your customer spend on clothing each month? What is the average amount he or she will spend on a sweater or jacket?

3. Open the disk that came with this book. Note: Since the information on the disk has been compressed, the files must be extracted onto the hard drive. You will need 4.3MB of memory to work with the files. Open the files directly into your particular paint program. Open the file named "Inspire" and describe the mood of the images. Do the images inspire any design idea? Do they inspire a particular palette? Can you imagine designing clothes for the customer you selected in the previous problem based on one of these images? What would the clothes look like?

4. Open the documents under "Theme." Select an image that would appeal to your customer. Use the image to think of a theme for a clothing category. Which clothing category would you select for your customer?

Chapter 5

Color

SCIENCE OR INTUITION?

Whether we look at a landscape, an interior space, a photograph, or a garment, the first thing human beings respond to is color. Color influences our emotional response to whatever we are looking at. It sets a mood. A color scheme can be seen as tranquil or exciting, cool or warm, feminine or masculine, neutral or bold, harmonious or cacophonous. It can lift the spirits of the viewer, soothe ruffled feelings, and evoke images and memories of places and events.

Most people have particular preferences for certain colors and color combinations, and often these color preferences are cultural and even geographical. People who live in hot, exotic climates often prefer bold, hot colors. People who live in strong ethnic environments tend to select colors based on what their particular culture considers beautiful. The definition of beauty changes not only from culture to culture, but also changes within a single culture over time.

The way people see individual colors varies greatly. Sensitivity to color depends on each person's physical, perceptual, and experiential makeup. Age plays an important role in perceiving variations among colors; over time, a person is less and less able to discriminate. An individual's experience also plays a great role in perceiving color. Twenty different people could consider 20 shades of green to be "lime" and who is to say which green is the correct "lime"?

In professional and artistic fields, as well as in everyday life, a person may be said to have a great "color sense." This usually means they put colors together in a creative, masterful way. This is a trait that is particular to them and uses perceptive, environmental, and experiential qualities. In a way, this sense can be called intuitive. Most artists and designers in the creative and applied arts have a feel for color that is enriched by schooling, but the basic propensity is intrinsic to that person.

Consider again the case of 20 people selecting the color that describes "lime." Certainly, there are instances when terminology and description of color in words is not satisfactory. A clear communication has to be created among people about the particular color "lime" that is being talked about. In professional situations, a scientific method of communicating color is necessary. In order to clearly communicate color, a number of different scientific systems have evolved.

COLOR SYSTEMS

Color classification can be broken down into a manageable process by defining a color based on three primary attributes. Then the color can be plotted on a graph and coded numerically. First, the attributes should be named.

Hue is another word for the name of the color. There are five principal hues on the color wheel: red, yellow, green, blue, and purple. There are five intermediate hues: yellow red, green yellow, blue green, purple blue, and red purple. Mixtures of hues create new hues. Red and yellow create orange, red and blue create violet, and so on. One hue blends into the next all the way around the color wheel. Adding white to a hue creates a tint; adding black creates a shade. Black, white, and grey have no hue, so they are called "neutral" colors.

Value, or lightness, is the shade of the color. It refers to how much white or black is mixed with the hue. The more black, the darker the shade; the more white, the lighter the shade. Two colors have the same value if they contain the same amount of white, black, or grey.

Chroma, or **saturation**, refers to the intensity of the color or the concentration of the hue. Chroma goes from dull to bright, from low to high, from subdued to brilliant. The more grey a color contains, the duller or less saturated it appears.

In 1905, Albert H. Munsell began codifying color based on its three attributes—hue, value, and chroma. He assigned numerical values based on the arrangement of the colors on his Munsell Color Tree. The Munsell color system is based on an established vertical axis that serves as the value scale. It goes from white to black in ten divisions. Next, the hues in the color wheel are arranged around the axis in ten horizontal increments based on chroma. The least saturated color is closest to the vertical axis and the most saturated color is on the perimeter. The Munsell system was the first organized way of addressing color. Later, each color in the system was numerically noted to express **hue, value, and chroma (HVC)** (see Figure 5–1 and Plate 12).

The Munsell system did not represent enough of the colors visible to the human eye and it relied on physical comparison with a master color. Since this measurement was left to the human eye, the drawbacks of perception and experience often

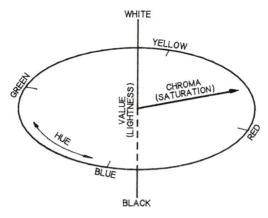

Figure 5–1 Simplified representation of color arrangement based on hue, value, and chroma (HVC) (Courtesy of X-Rite®, Inc.)

did not allow for complete accuracy. It was, however, the basis for establishing a system for thinking about color and is still the most widely used method for learning about the properties of color.

In 1931, the Commission Internationale de l'Eclairage established a mathematical system for defining a color space, or a notated system. The CIE system involves the numerical measurement of reflected light based on the response of the "average person" or standard observer to varying wavelengths. The CIE system was updated in 1976 (see Plate 13). Later, other color spaces and numerical expressions of color like CIELAB and CIELUV were established (see Figure 5–2). These systems use instruments to compare the colors of two different subjects. These instruments are known as colorimeters, densitometers, and spectrophotometers.

Measuring color requires that the colors being analyzed be seen under controlled conditions. The three types of light—fluorescent, incandescent, or daylight—have a great effect on color, and unless the color matching is always done under the same light condition, a great variation in the results is possible. In industry, this situation is controlled through the use of a light box. **Light boxes** create a stable environment in which to measure a color sample. They are cubelike units that can illuminate the color sample with any type of desired light; shadows are controlled, as is background color, two factors that can affect the outcome. Most of the time, a light box relies on the human eye for color discrimination. This may take a great deal of time, but the results are usually acceptable if the designer or colorist has keen color perception.

When absolute, precise color control is important, **colorimeters**, **spectrophotometers**, and **densitometers** are used (see Figure 5–3). Industries that produce paint or other color media rely on this precision, as does the textile and apparel industry. When design and production of clothing is sometimes spread out around the entire world, exact color communication is vital. This will be discussed further in the next sections.

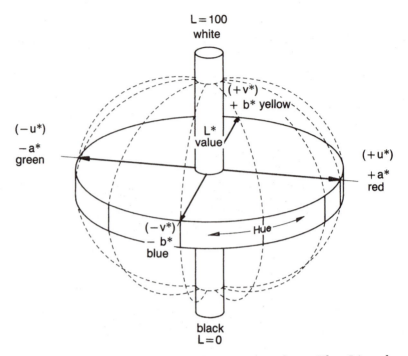

Figure 5–2 3-D representation of CIELAB colors. The L* value is represented on the center axis. The a* and b* axes appear on the horizontal plane. (Courtesy of X-Rite®, Inc.)

WORKING WITH COLOR

Designers and colorists work with color in one of two ways: using pigment or using light. When a designer uses paint or dye to visualize and mix colors, he or she is working with a **subtractive color** process (see Figure 5–4). This means that the net color

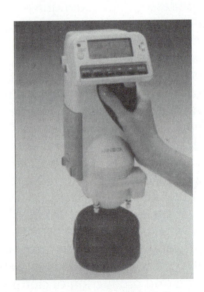

Figure 5–3 Spectrophotometers analyze color and provide numeric formulas so color can be coded (Courtesy of Minolta Corp.)

reflected back to the eye is the result of all other colors being absorbed or subtracted by the ink on the page or the dye on the fabric. In subtractive color, all colors mixed together yield black. This means that if all of the primary colors were mixed on a page they would all be absorbed or subtracted by the page and under ideal conditions, we would see black reflected back to us.

In the subtractive color model, the primary colors are **cyan, magenta, yellow, and black,** or **CMYK.** These are called **process colors** because they are used in the printing process. They can be combined in various ways to produce all the colors in the spectrum. This system is used by printers and dyers to achieve pigment color for a wide variety of products.

When designers use light to create color, as is the case in all computer imaging, an entirely different system of color mixing is used. Monitors display the "primary" colors of **red, green, and blue,** or **RGB.** All colors mixed together create white. This is called the **additive color** model (see Figure 5–5). It is important to note that when experimenting with color on a computer screen, equal

SUBTRACTIVE COLOR

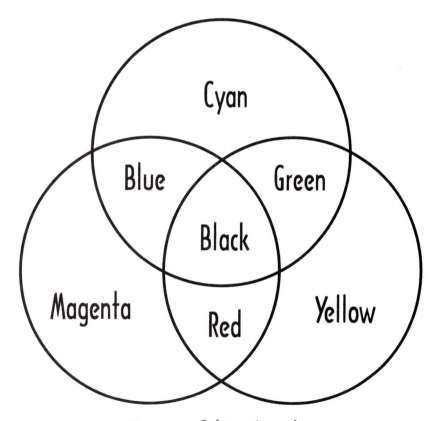

Figure 5–4   Subtractive color

intensities of primary colors must be mixed together to produce new colors.

A designer working on a computer is usually interested in seeing what color might look like when it is printed, which is the CMYK mode rather than the RGB shown on the screen. Computers can simulate the CMYK color mode by translating from the RGB colors. In this translation, the computer assigns each pixel a percentage value for each of the process colors. Most computer programs allow the user to set both the RGB and CMYK colors by number. But don't be confused. Even though the CMYK mode is simulated on screen, you are still looking at color created by light rather than pigment—that is, in the RGB mode.

The mathematically notated CIELAB color system mentioned previously is also incorporated into many computer programs. The advantage of using this system, which incorporates all colors including CMYK and RGB, is that consistent documents can be created regardless of the type of computer, monitor, software program, or printer. Other modes exist, but are not used as often as the three mentioned here.

Understanding the Color Wheel

A good designer will have established a framework for working with color before applying that knowledge to a product. As mentioned earlier, some of this response to color is instinctive. But experimenting with that instinct requires some basic theory. Understanding the color wheel is the beginning of the process (see Plate 14). Applying value and chroma to the hues on the color wheel is the next step. Designers learn to modify hue with value and chroma, and in time they learn to quickly discriminate dirty color from clean, light from bright, and so on.

In addition to discrimination, this experimentation ultimately teaches control over color and provides the ability to manipulate it according to the goals of the project. Looking at the color wheel in terms of the temperature of colors is a start. Warm hues go from red to yellow, orange, and pink, and include brown and burgundy on the color wheel. Cool colors go from green to purple and include blue and some greys.

In order to play with colors, a designer has to select the medium: either pigment or light. Both systems allow for experimentation and investigation. The Albers color theory course, based on the book, *Interaction of Color*,[21] uses pigmented paper or computer visualization to offer ways of understanding and manipulating color. The most important aspect of studying color is the relationship of colors to each other. Some colors blend into each other and offer no contrast; others vibrate when put next to each other. Some provide too much contrast. This learning is experiential—you have to see the relationships to understand them.

ADDITIVE COLOR

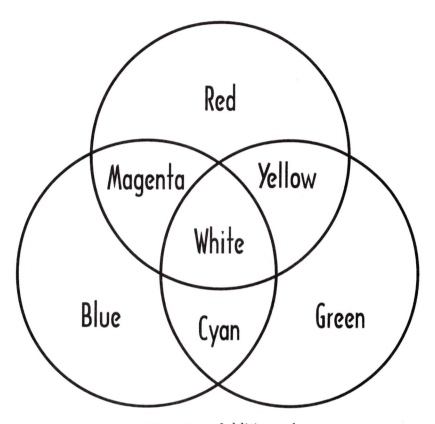

Figure 5–5   Additive color

Analogous colors are any shades, tints, or tones of color that are at 90 degree angles on the color wheel. Since two analogous colors share some of their color, they tend to blend nicely, but still offer some interest or tension. Examples are red and orange, or blue and purple.

Achromatic color combinations include black, white, or grey as one of the colors. These almost always look well together.

Complementary colors are on opposite sides of the color wheel. Red and green, orange and blue, yellow and purple are all complementary colors. Each pair of colors is a complement because between them they contain all the colors on the color wheel. When bright, complementary colors are put next to each other, they tend to vibrate and the edges between them become blurry. When a hue and its complement are mixed, they neutralize each other and create a muddy grey or brownish color.

Contrasting colors have three colors between them on the color wheel. Examples are red and blue violet, purple and blue green.

Secondary colors are created by mixing two primary colors: red and yellow produce orange; blue and yellow produce green.

Tertiary colors are produced by mixing a primary color with a secondary color. An example is red mixed with orange which yields red orange.

It is important to note that all hues of red remain in the same family no matter how much value and chroma is adjusted. In other words, pink is still a red hue as is burgundy. When combining colors, all of the possible varieties within a family of hues can be combined with all of the possible varieties within another family of hues. This results in endless possible color combinations. For example, in working with the complementary colors of orange and blue, any shade and/or intensity of orange can be combined with any shade and/or intensity of blue and the pair will still be complementary. Any hue that is combined with another member of its own family, lighter or darker or with more or less intensity, will tend to harmonize well together.

Through experience, a designer will learn how to work with color in combination, how to tone down a color that "pops," how to create balance and harmony, how to make a color statement that is bold and young in spirit, how to make color recede or come to the foreground. Since a great deal of a designer's work life is spent editing personal work or the work of others, the language of color—words such as *value, intensity, tint,* and so forth—provide the best way to critique and modify a visual product.

Color and the Apparel Industry

Selecting color for apparel is both a highly creative and scientifically specific process. We know that a designer comes up with a theme or a point of view for a line early in the conceptual stage. Sometimes color plays a strong role in inspiring the theme. The colors of fall foliage or Caribbean waters could set the framework for a color story. But color selection is not a mystery, left to the whim of the designer. Color direction for a season is initiated by organizations such as the Color Association of the United States (CAUS) and the International Color Authority (ICA). Experts from all segments of the apparel industry gather to predict and recommend seasonal color for fibers, yarns, and fabric. These forecasts are available nearly two years ahead of the selling season.

Cotton Incorporated, the Wool Bureau, International Linen Promotion Council, and others offer projections, maintain libraries, and give formal presentations to designers and companies who subscribe to them or are licensees of their organizations. They are trade associations that represent the primary marketplace: fiber and yarn producers and mills. They establish their color projections, often in concert with CAUS and ICA. Fiber and yarn producers such as Hoechst Celanese, Burlington, Dupont, and Monsanto also make their own projections and somehow achieve a level of similarity and consistency in the industry (see Plate 15). This is why in any particular season many companies are showing similar palettes. Color is cyclical; that is, a color such as purple will be popular for a period of time and then will recede in importance, only to return a few years later. Forecasters and color experts keep track of color, they follow historical patterns of color popularity. Sometimes they predict that dusty colors will be important. Sometimes they predict that clear tints will be important. The predictions are based on scientific study. Designers then have a base from which to work when selecting a seasonal palette for their companies.

Other color forecasting services such as Promostyl, Colorbox, Huepoint, Pat Tunsky, Inc., and many others work directly with designers and manufacturers on a service-for-fee basis. These companies create a standard palette for each season based on approximately 50 total colors, as shown in Plate 16. These are usually divided into categories of color.

> *Brights* are colors that are clear and saturated; they are not muddied with grey and appear on the perimeter of the Munsell Tree.
>
> *Darks* are shades of various hues that are deepened with black. They appear on the lower part of the vertical axis on the Munsell Tree.
>
> *Pastels* are hues that are lightened or tinted with white. They appear on the upper part of the vertical axis on the Munsell Tree.
>
> *Midtones* are the colors between dark and pastel. Since most colors are mid tone, they are the most frequently used colors. More than one group of midtones often appear in a color forecast.
>
> *Neutrals* are colors that have low intensity. They can be light or dark, but they have low chroma and are located close to the vertical axis on the Munsell Tree.
>
> *Accent colors* are offered as a way to add life, brightness, or contrast to the overall palette.

These categories are usually given an alluring title rather than simply being called pastels, brights, or darks. Thematic terminology is used: for example, a group of neutral colors can be based on hues of stone and could be labeled "masonry."

Designers select from among the seasonal palette colors based on specific considerations:

> *Mood or Theme*—refers to the overall feeling of the group or line. If the theme of a group is inspired by Navajo Indian cul-

ture and artifacts, the palette can be made up of the bright colors found in Indian costume, or the colors that are found in Navajo pottery.

Clothing category—refers to the major apparel divisions and subdivisions. The colors chosen for a menswear product will probably differ from the palette used in womenswear and childrenswear. A palette developed for junior sportswear will usually differ from a palette for career sportswear for women in the bridge price point.

Function—refers to the particular activity or purpose that the clothing will be worn for. Swimwear and active sportswear will usually have a bold, bright, graphic palette, whereas lingerie will include pastels with some brights. The intended end use of the clothing helps to determine the palette.

Price point—refers to the cost of the garment. Often the price of the final product will have a bearing on the palette. Designing clothing at the couture or even designer level allows for wide experimentation and color expression. In the moderate men's category, a target customer would not ordinarily be happy with fuschia trousers, but at the designer level, there is a chance. . . .

Keeping all of these points in mind, the designer will interpret the mood or theme of the group using colors from the palette. Many designers use a forecaster's palette as a guide and then create their own color stories for their particular companies. Again, at the couture level, there is a lot of latitude and high-end designers use color for experimentation in ways that those in mass production cannot.

In planning a color story, a designer has to keep in mind that certain colors are favored and expected by the consumer of that product. Customers may have clear preferences for color that are maintained over time and perform well at the retail level. For example, in childrenswear, the girls size 4–6X category requires that there be some pink and purple hues. These are the best-selling colors in that category, customers expect them, and they should be part of the color story. However, the way the designer expresses the requisite colors is open to great variation. The color pink can be a clear, bright, intense pink or a light, pastel pink or a toned-down, greyed-out pink that is more dusty and subtle. In menswear, blue is a traditionally, good seller, so a designer will always include a variety of blues in the palette for most men's products.

The designer also has to decide how the colors will be selected and arranged for the textiles in the line as well as the way the colors will be arranged when those textiles appear on a body. For the most part, a designer will select colors that go into the **bottom-weight fabrics** (those that are cut into the jackets, pants, skirts, and sometimes dresses); the colors that will become **top weights** (blouses, tops, and sometimes dresses); and those that will be **novelties,** which include prints and special weaves and/or knits. In doing this, the designer is establishing a relationship among the palette colors and a way that the final clothes will appear on the body. (Color and textiles are discussed in greater detail in Chapter 6.)

The way colors work together on the body is often a trend issue. Color for women's sportswear separates for a particular season might be based on a monochromatic viewpoint. This means that a single hue is selected and then the color is varied in terms of tint or shade. In an ensemble, the pants could be walnut brown, the jacket could be a doeskin color, and the blouse might be beige. Another example of a monochromatic theme could be pieces done in variations of white arranged together in a group.

Other possibilities include an analogous color story or a complementary color story. Color blocking is often a trendy direction in apparel design, or a designer could use black with a variety of brights. Bright color could be used with light color, or a medley of darks or pastels or neutral colors with bright accents is possible. It all depends on a designer's point of view and the direction decided upon by the design and merchandising teams.

Communicating Color

Once color is finalized, the design team has to communicate its color selections to all phases of design, production, and sales. Forecasting services provide their customers with yarn samples of color as well as paper color cards. But it is much easier to perceive textile color though yarn samples or fabric color swatches. The design team has to be certain that their color choices can be communicated to the mills producing the textiles and that the dyes are as close as possible to the original selections. A line of clothing can be produced at a number of different locations throughout the world. For example, in a group of coordinated sportswear separates, the bottom weights can come from a company in South Carolina, the prints for blouses could be made in Japan, and the sweaters could be knitted in China. All of these garments could have the same shipping date and would have to arrive at the company's warehouse at the same time and in colors that are an exact match. Obviously, color is a critical issue. If the color in the sweater does not match the print in the blouse or the solid in the pants, the group can't be shipped, the delivery date will be missed, and the entire order could be canceled. Any manufacturer would want to avoid this loss of revenue; thus, great care and expense go into color controls and standards.

Color standards for the American textile industry have been established by the National Bureau of Standards in Washington, DC, and the Color Association of the United States. CIELAB's numerically based standards described earlier offer a means of regulating color communication in any language. Pantone, a company that serves color-matching needs across numerous industries offers a textile color system that is used widely in the apparel industry (see Figure 5–6). A paper or cotton swatch of each color in the PANTONE TEXTILE Color System® is sold and every color is numerically coded in six digits which relate to hue, value, and saturation. In this way, numbers become the color identifiers and communication among manufacturing sites in different parts of the world becomes less of an obstacle. **Lab dips** and check systems for color matching are still required, but the numeric systems cut down on the amount of times samples have to be presented for approval and correction. In the apparel industry, a designer will include numeric information about color on the computerized textile specifications sheets. This makes the specs available to anyone in the design and production process and makes the management of color feasible. As we mentioned in Chapter 3, technology is becoming available which offers the designer an instant dye recipe for any color selected. This recipe can accompany the design through to production, making color matching easier.

Color and the Digital World

A computer is capable of displaying more than 16 million different colors. The human eye can only see a small proportion of this vast number. But it is truly a designer's dream to have such a vast palette for experimentation and play. Mixing color on a comput-

Figure 5–6   PANTONE TEXTILE Color System® (Courtesy of Pantone, Inc.)

er screen is based on the additive color process described earlier. The color produced by light is different from the color produced by pigment. Since ink is pigment, the color seen on the computer screen is never quite the same as the color printed onto a page. In addition, different types of paper used by the printer offer differing results. Maintaining color integrity from screen to printout has been one of the greatest challenges in computer-generated design work.

Color for Visualization versus Color for Production

A designer will work at a computer developing a palette and designing textile prints or weaves. Often the final output is a presentation board that is shared among the design, merchandising, and sales personnel. Sometimes a private label designer will work with a customer in front of the computer in order to modify color or visualize a particular stripe or print on a garment silhouette. Sometimes a group of designers will gather around a terminal for a critique of someone's work. In all of these cases the image on the screen is used to present an idea or direction and to provide visualization of an idea. The color used is for viewing purposes only and will not be used by technicians who mix the dyes used for textile printing and production.

Color that provides technical information to the mill, to the factory, or to the converter who is engraving and printing the fabric has to be precise and scientifically correct. If a digital image is printed and this printout is used as a sample by the mill for production, then the computer and the printer must be **calibrated** to match each other. Calibration refers to the setting of controls from computer to computer (or printer) so that color among screens or between screen and printer matches. If a disk is used to transfer information from the design room to the mill, the computer screens should be calibrated.

When communication between and among computers is necessary for either viewing or production, the terminals are networked or linked together so that information can be shared within an office or around the world. These situations are more and more common in today's industry, and computers that share information along with the printers that create hard copy have to be calibrated.

In simplified terms, calibrating a monitor to the printer means that the RGB colors that appear on the screen have to be made to match the CMYK colors used in the printing process. Devices such as the PANTONE® ColorDrive™ system will calibrate color between screen and output device under any color system: CMYK, RGB, a variety of PANTONE Color Systems, CIE, HLS, and even spectral data. Other calibration utilities are on the market, but consistent results are best achieved with software measurement devices such as colorimeters and spectrophotometers. Most designers at the time of this writing are still using the manual, hand/eye matching methods which can be accomplished by anyone, albeit at a great expense of time.

In order to match a screen palette to a printer palette, you must create a document with many splotches of various colors. Since each RGB or CMYK has an exact numerical representation, precision can be maintained by making note of color numbers for each splotch provided by the computer program you are working with. This step is vital. Print out the colors, but don't be surprised that they look nothing like the screen version. Select from among the printed colors those that match your original palette. You will have numerical codes for each of them so you can select these when working on screen. It will take some time to adjust to using what appear to be "incorrect" colors on the screen, but they will then print according to the expected palette.

When calibrating monitor to monitor, the RGB colors have to be made to appear the same on all the monitors in the network. The lighting in the room has an effect on color as does the length of time since the monitors were turned on. A computer usually needs 30 minutes to stabilize. The room should be free of external light and the brightness and contrast adjustments should be matched between screens and not moved again unless another adjustment is necessary. The goal in calibration is to adjust grey tones so there is no color cast to them. Many software instruction manuals provide calibration instructions, so the reader is directed to those resources.

Photo credit: Laura Satori

Interview with Hilary Spalding Fischer
Designer, Hartstrings, Inc.

Fischer: Hartstrings is a company that produces coordinated children's sportswear. We are a multimillion-dollar company with distributors throughout the United States. Our national office is in New

York City in the children's wear mart on 34th Street and we also have international representation. I started working for Hartstrings ten years ago after working for another children's wear company. I started as an assistant designer, working for Peggy Hart Earl, who is the president, owner, and head designer. Within a year, I was doing all the development of artwork, helping to develop custom fabric prints, designing all of the accessory items, and then doing all the brochure artwork.

R.W.C.:   What type of brochure do you produce?

Fischer: Hartstrings is unusual in the industry in that we put out a detailed brochure that we offer to our buyers. Every item we produce is depicted in line form and in color along with a full photographic spread that captures the spirit of each different group that we do.

R.W.C.:   Do you use a computer to develop the brochure?

Fischer: We started working on the computer four years ago. Prior to that, I was doing all of the line drawings by hand and each season we produced six girls' groups of approximately twenty items per group and six boy's groups of approximately twenty items per group. I drew all of the silhouettes by hand and colored them in, trying to render the scale of the prints. We would then duplicate those for in-house use. I had the responsibility of painting them myself or contracting an artist to paint them so they could be photographed for the brochure. In 1991, we started using the computer, and we knew immediately when we began that the most direct application for us would be for the brochure.

R.W.C.:   How does your company use the brochure?

Fischer: The brochures go to every buyer prior to the release of the line. So the buyer receives the brochure, they peruse it, and then they call their sales rep or regional manager and make an appointment to review the line. So, it's a huge plus for them because they get a chance to preview what we have to sell.

R.W.C.:   Do you also do technical renderings for print design on the computer?

Fischer: Because of the program that we use, our contractors do the technical specifications from our artwork. For example, for Holiday, I might render a black watch plaid in exact scale and color for production on a 6.5-ounce brushed flannel. We would send the computer-generated artwork to one of our contractors; the choice would depend upon which mill could give us the best production at the best price on a timely basis.

R.W.C.:   Would you say then that you use the computer primarily for representational purposes when designing fabrics?

Fischer: Yes. For our purposes, the computer provides an opportunity for Peggy, who is the owner and head designer, to have more control over the output of the line. She needs fewer designers reporting to her because we can get more work produced in a shorter period of time by using the computer. The initial rendering takes time, but once you have the basic skeleton of a black watch plaid, if you wanted fewer bands of navy, or if you wanted to change green to purple, it can happen immediately. That's really where the time-saving factor comes in.

R.W.C.:   Do your salespeople show the computerized fabric renderings to buyers for their reaction?

Fischer: That is usually the way it happens in other companies, but in our company we don't usually show the line to any of the buyers. We show it to our sales reps and they tend to have an understanding of how their buyers will react. Because our whole line is traditional, classic, coordinated sportswear, we don't follow fashion trends very heavily. So, while mohair might have been very big for the high end of the children's wear business last year, it wasn't something we would ever touch. A little bit too fashion forward for us. So, the issues that we discuss (with the sales reps) are: Can we do this stone mixed with brown and jade for boys, or is that too risky? Do we like the idea of doing an apple motif again, followed directly on the coattails of a spring cherry group and holiday strawberry group? The questions can get down to silhouettes or trim items—ball fringe that has to be cast aside because it looks too trendy. Generally, we ask if the sales reps understand the group—if the teapots, teacups, and saucers mixed with a cabbage rose floral works. If the sales staff doesn't get it, we're not going to do it. We'll come up with something else that is more easily accepted, because we found that if the director of sales and head of merchandising don't understand it, we don't sell it.

R.W.C.:   What process do you use to develop silhouettes?

Fischer: Years ago, I started transposing all of the little flat silhouettes that I had in my files into my computer. I have established a library with a few thousand illustrations that I have done that are all coordinated to scale, so they work with each other. You could pull up a V-neck cardigan or a cardigan vest or a roll-neck tunic sweater and they all have similar proportions. So that if you put them with a lycra legging body, they would all work. Because it's children's wear, we aren't into high fashion illustration on the computer. It's really more of a line drawing, flat sketch effect, which works beautifully in house and the buyers have come to understand exactly what they see. It doesn't require a lot of interpretation.

R.W.C.:   Do the buyers select the silhouettes right from the brochure?

Fischer: Our buyers usually receive the brochure and go to one of our showrooms to see the line. We have had people write in orders sight unseen, but generally we are a large part of most of our customers volume and they do tend to come in and see the line. The other benefit in having this brochure is that they can take it home with them, figure what their open to buy is, what else they've purchased from others, and have all of these flat silhouette sketches to jog their memory.

R.W.C.:   Which program do you use and how did you select it?

Fischer: Well, that's a very interesting story. We had a general manager who had realized the applications of the computer in his previous job. He had been in packaging, and had used CAD for product development. He encouraged Peggy to consider it for assisting in the design process. So she looked at all of the businesses in the greater New York area that were producing paint and graphics software packages as well as high-end apparel programs. Most of the software programs were very complicated. Peggy wanted a tool which was an augmentation of the process, and not something which would put the entire business on hold for six months until everybody was up and running. Ultimately, the program that we wound up with turned out to be a $100 PC graphics package. It was an animated paint program which was used to design and to develop video games. It was very user friendly, with an exposed palette and simple but suitable tools and functions. We had the software modified slightly to meet our needs. The person (at the time), who was our general manager was also our CAD trainer and the three of us—Peggy, a sweater designer, and myself—sat shoulder to shoulder and learned by hook or by crook. It was truly baptism by fire because we had to design the line on this new computer in a very tight time frame. With every mistake we made, we learned something and it didn't take us long to get things under control.

R.W.C.:   What type of printing system do you use?

Fischer: We have a Hewlett Packard jet printer. However, our program has a very remedial resolution and it is not what most people would want to use for publishing. As an in-house tool, it is great. I think the time is coming when we will have to invest in newer technology once again, so that we can print all of our artwork in house. The complications of having printing done outside is that you have to have someone extremely proficient at analyzing computer-generated color on a color copier or you never duplicate the color well enough. And color is such a key part of what we do— the green on the boy's black watch plaid page must match the green in the girl's apple page.

R.W.C.:   How do you deal with the matching problems from screens to printers?

Fischer: Well, we used to try to. First of all, I have established about 200 color standards that we use regularly. So everyone has a nice color palette which they keep by the computer and all the numbers are indicated. Navy in our palette is 36-0-55; red is 100-14-0. All of the 200 colors are relatively consistent from printer to printer here. As far as adjusting the screen so that what we see on screen is truly accurate, we tried for a while to do that, but we got realistic and decided we know what that color looks like, we have to trust when it prints out it will look that way. As long as someone has the ability to adjust their monitor on site, color will never be consistent. And screen consistency really doesn't matter in our case because our color standards remain the same from season to season. Our navy does not change. In a company where navy varies, it would be a critical issue to deal with. For us, it is not.

R.W.C.:   How do you plan your color and print direction for a season?

Fischer: Since we design and manufacture traditional, classic sportswear, much of what we do by way of color and print direction is repetitive seasonally. It is relative to previously successful groupings. For example, red and navy is always an important color combination for us in the fall season. As far as prints go, we try to keep things simple, clean, not too fussy. As far as the children's wear industry goes, I think color really is all over the place. In the moderate side, the mass market, color is very fashion oriented, it's very fashion driven. There are always primaries and there are always pastels. But, I think today, the neutrals—the blacks and grays and the heathered tones—are really becoming much more meaningful in children's wear. I think in general, the consumer is more sophisticated and I think businesses like the Gap and Esprit have as much to do with affecting color palettes in the children's wear industry as anything. Certainly in the Gap's case, they had women's wear and men's wear to draw from. So they were really forging new boundaries, new horizons in terms of color. And I think they helped the industry in general take that leap from pale pink, pale blue, mint green, and pale yellow to maybe some corals and olives that might have been perceived as controversial 20 years ago, but are now standard.

R.W.C.:   Hartstrings is known for their signature prints. Are they all developed in house or do you buy work at print shows or from mills?

Fischer: Of all the prints that we do in the girls' line, almost 50 percent are custom prints. In the boys' line, almost 100 percent are custom prints. We usually don't buy work done on the outside, unless it's an exclusive arrangement. We do have a very good relationship with one print house and they know our look well enough to know if they are previewing an artist's work, and this artist has something that is in the vein of Hartstrings, they would buy it, send it to us, and say, "We purchased this with you in mind, are you interested in doing this?"

R.W.C.:   What are your sources of inspiration?

Fischer: We get our inspiration from everywhere. Almost everywhere we go, there is something we see that is exciting to us and inspires us. Peggy was in New England visiting her family, and she went into a craftsman's guild and saw a charming little Christmas ornament. That became a motif for last Holiday. We also maintain inspiration files, I have drawers full, and no matter where I am, I am constantly cutting things out and saving things. Sometimes Peggy will come to me with a concept. She'll say she's interested in seeing a particular motif in print. I'll refer to my files for inspiration and then begin rendering different options for her approval. She can watch me as I work on the computer and our computers are interfaced. As soon as I save an image, she can load it up and adjust it herself or suggest changes.

R.W.C.:	What type of editing process do you go through when presenting your computer-generated ideas?
Fischer:	We have a number of design presentations each season. Initially, just to get the core feelings of the groups. Later, things are adjusted, balanced, fine-tuned on the computer. Finally, they are presented for the last review. Once the groups are approved, we print them and use them internally for developmental purposes. Ultimately, these pages become the artwork pages for our brochure.
R.W.C.:	What path did you follow before arriving at this design position?
Fischer:	I went to Dartmouth College and majored in art. When I graduated, I went to work for Macy's in New York City in their retail management program. When I left there, I ended up going into children's wear manufacturing for a very small company called Freitag. I originally worked in sales, but a month into it they acquired the license to manufacture and distribute the Marimekko label. They needed someone who could make patterns, make first samples, and work with designers in the studio and also with the buyers in the showroom. I knew how to sew and I had a rough idea about patternmaking, so I got the job. Then I went to Parson's, took classes in fashion illustration and in patternmaking to augment my background. My industry experience, the training I had in sales, marketing, and retail coupled with my own innate abilities was enough to finally convince people I could do the job. It took me a while to really recognize that design was really what I wanted to do. Once I got there, I knew that that was the place I wanted to be.

STUDY QUESTIONS AND PROBLEMS

1. Name the color systems used by the software you are using.
2. What are the difficulties in matching color from computer screen to printout? How does the designer try to resolve these problems?
3. Use the image you selected from the "Inspire" folder in Chapter 4. Create a seven-color palette based on this image using computer-generated color tabs. List the numerical components of each of the seven colors using the color system used by your software (PANTONE Color System, RGB, and CMYK). Save your new palette. Print it out and compare your print color to screen color. Describe the process you would use to match the color more closely.
4. Open an image under the "Theme" folder. Reduce the number of colors in the image to seven. Substitute the new palette you created in problem 3 for the palette in this image.
5. Open the "Palettes" folder and the "Seasonal" document. Create a ten-color palette for menswear and save it. Create a ten-color palette for childrenswear and a ten-color palette for womenswear.

Remember the customer images you selected in Chapter 4, problem 2, and select these palettes for them.

6. Use one of the "Theme" images. Select a category of clothing and a palette created in the previous problem and describe a clothing category for your customer.

7. Experiment with the palette to create a monochromatic color story, an analogous color story, a bright story, and a pastel story. Save each of them as separate documents. Remember to indicate the numerical identification for each.

Chapter 6

Fabric: The Designer's Medium

Textiles are the medium from which apparel is created. A designer's experience with a wide variety of fabrics and an understanding of their characteristics is vital to the design process. A designer has to know how different fabrics perform: how they feel when handled, how they drape when hung over a body, how they move with the wearer. A lovely sketch can only come to life if the fabric selection is appropriate for the design.

Each sketch that a designer completes must include a clear communication of the fabric that will be used to realize the design. A swatch of the intended fabric goes much farther than words in helping to understand a sketch; it can be handled, the actual color can be appreciated, and something about the drape of the fabric can be envisioned. With experience, a designer can leave the swatch out and verbally indicate the type of fabric to be used. This is possible because the designer has developed an image and frame of reference for many types of fabrics and how they perform.

When the design for a fabric is a print, a computer printout can provide a good indication of the pattern. When this is combined with a description of the cloth that the pattern will be printed on, the buyer or merchandiser will be able to visualize the product quickly and easily. However, a computer cannot provide the designer with the tactile quality that fabric in hand can offer. There is no escaping the need to hold the fabric, to hang it over the shoulder of a dress form or a model, or to experiment with tailoring it or stretching it around a three-dimensional form. Forecasters predict that technology will someday be able to mimic fabric drape; the designer will be able to specify the type and weight of fabric to the computer, which will then offer a drape simulation. Presently, only stretch fabrics for foundation garments and swimwear are able to be draped by the computer, but researchers have made strides toward computer draping of wovens.

Certain industry-specific CAD programs allow the designer to select or create yarns and to weave, on screen, almost any weave configuration. Prints can also be created and be put into repeat instantly and a weave type assigned. The color of the print can be manipulated and experimented with in myriad ways in moments. Colorways can be established and seen quickly. In the past, each time a designer wanted to see a garment with some color change, the painting had to be redone by hand, often taking hours or even days to complete. Now the textile can be finalized, the silhouette created, and a complete visualization presented in a very short time.

THE FABRIC SELECTION PROCESS

How does a designer and/or a merchandiser begin to develop the direction for the fabrication of a line? What are the resources available to him or her and what are the primary considerations that have to be weighed during the early stages of this process?

As mentioned earlier in the text, designers subscribe to trend and forecasting services so at the outset they know something about the textile predictions for the upcoming season. They will have gained a sense of new trends: whether textural fabrics or print will be important. They will know if the trend for stretch characteristics in fabrics will continue or if sheers will be important. Fiber companies are the earliest predictors of trends because they work two years in advance of the season. Textile trade magazines such as *Textile World, Knitting Times Magazine,* and *America's Textile International* are valuable, along with textile libraries maintained by trade organizations such as Cotton Inc. and the Wool Bureau. These libraries offer members of their organizations the opportunity to look at large holdings of current fabric swatches from a great array of mills. Occasionally, these organizations, as well as trend and forecasting service companies, offer tours and presentations to students.

Fabric shows such as IFFE, Interstoff, the Yarn Fair, Ideacomo, Texitalia, Jardins d'Elegance, and Premiere Vision are invaluable resources for the designer. There they learn about new fabrics and fibers and gain the opportunity to experience the hand of the new fabrics. Shows such as Interstoff allow designers to see fabrics that are being created in various parts of the world, rather than just in their own marketplaces. Many times, inspiration for a line comes directly from the fabric, so the study of textiles both old and new should be an ongoing part of every designer's education. Many museums and universities have textile libraries that designers can use for inspiration.

Print shows and print houses are another resource for designers. A company may purchase art or **croquis** of prints created by textile artists. The company can then have these designs put into repeat and used for their lines. Organized print shows such as

Surtex, Imprints, and the Print Show are places where designers can look at and purchase the work of textile artists.

Copyright infringement and piracy have become big issues in the apparel industry because computers can quickly modify an existing print that may belong to a textile artist. Print piracy, which is the commercial use of an artist's work without permission, is unlawful and a designer should always keep the ethics of the industry in mind and maintain personal integrity as well as that of the company. Another artist's work should not be "borrowed" unless the rights to the work have been secured.

Other considerations of great importance in starting to think about the fabrics for a line are both aesthetic and practical:

1. Is the fabric *aesthetically pleasing*? The first response that a designer or a customer has to fabric is based on the senses. Color, which was discussed in Chapter 5, is the first element the viewer experiences. Next is the pattern or print of the fabric, and finally the feel, or hand, of the fabric. The first thing a shopper does after absorbing information about color is touch the fabric—to feel it against the skin. A positive tactile experience is a very high expectation with most consumers and should not be underestimated. If the fabric is appealing to the senses, then all the questions about practicality and function can be raised.

2. What is the *target market* and the *price point* of the garment? Who is the customer? Obviously, the same fabric will not be selected when designing children's clothing as when designing sportswear for the bridge market. If the target market is the junior sportswear category, the price per yard of the fabric has to be in a certain range in order to produce a final product that will stay within that range. Goods at $10 per yard will result in a garment that is way over the acceptable price point for the junior market segment. A designer will usually know what price range to stay within when looking for fabrics.

3. What *season* is the design for? Wool usually won't work for a spring/summer line, and maybe a heavy brushed cotton twill won't work either. The weight of the fabric is very important and the designer should make sure that an appropriate match is made between the season and the weight of the fabric intended for the line.

4. Does the company have a *look* or image to maintain? Often the textiles and prints that a company uses become part of the image of the company. Laura Ashley is an example, as is Giorgio Armani.

5. What is the *end use* of the fabric? What type of function will the final garment fulfill? Will the garment be comfortable and appropriate for that function? If the clothing will be used for active sports such as skiing or fitness, the fabric has

to stretch and recover, breathe, and be comfortable. If the designs will become evening dresses to be worn for dancing or a party, the fabric has to be festive, sensuous, or elegant.

6. Is the method of *care* and *maintenance* of the fabric appropriate for the design category? When designing children's clothes, for example, the designer has to be aware that the clothes will be washed over and over again. The fabric has to be easy to care for, that is, machine washable and dryable. On the other hand, in the designer market, dry cleaning is expected and accepted.

7. Are there any *production considerations* that have to be taken into account? Does the fabric require special machinery or handling? Does the company's production facility have the necessary machinery in house or will new resources have to be established which might cost time and money?

A designer or a design assistant will spend time in the market about a year ahead of the season, looking for new products in the textile area. Besides the fabric shows, they will shop the textile market, go to the various showrooms to see new lines, and set up appointments for mill representatives to visit their design studios. If a certain fabric seems interesting, the designer will sample it and the mill will send a **mill end**, which is usually two to three yards for the designer to experiment with.

Usually the designer goes into the marketplace with a preestablished idea about the direction for the season that has been discussed with the merchandising team. Together the design and merchandising teams have come up with a theme and a color story. When the market search for new fabric ideas begins, it is much easier to have these parameters to start from rather than searching the textile market without definite direction. Once swatches and ideas have been gathered, designers and merchandisers work together to edit the fabrics and to come up with plans for the final fabrication for the new season.

ORGANIZING THE FABRICS

Usually, a number of different types of fabric make up a line. The myriad types and constructions of woven and knitted fabrics would make up a volume in itself; so without delving too far into the technical makeup of textiles, it is important to note that a designer should be very fluent with this aspect of the industry. A designer can study many good references to learn about weave constructions, knitting, and printing processes, along with industrial terminology. It is crucial that the designer understand as much as possible about textile production, its limitations and parameters. A designer should be fluent in regard to fabric types and identification. He or she should know the difference between faille and ottoman and the difference between jersey and inter-lock.

In broad, general terms, fabrics can be broken down by weight in relationship to their end uses. For example, consider the development of fabrication for a sportswear group. The fabric weight needed for the pants, skirts, and jackets in a sportswear story are referred to as **bottom weights**. Bottom-weight fabrics are heavier than the fabric used for the blouses and soft separates in the same group. These lighter-weight fabrics are called top weights. Sometimes the term **top weight** can be interchanged with *dress weight* for that part of the market. *Suitings* and *coating weight* fabrics, along with *shirtings*, are also available to designers and manufacturers of those products. Normally, the weights of the various fabrics are measured in ounces per yard; so a 10-ounce piece of goods means that one yard of the fabric weighs 10 ounces.

Sometimes, certain fabrics are used over and over again by a company. For example, a childrenswear company may use a particular cotton rib season after season. This rib becomes a *staple* in the line and is used over and over again even though the color may change. Many items in a line are made of staple, or basic, fabrics such as wool crepe or cotton twill, and are used by a company season after season. A designer will establish contacts with the suppliers and converters of their staples so each new season does not mean a completely new market search.

Yarn dyes are important in sportswear (and in suits and coats) and they are woven plaids or stripes and tweeds. They are called yarn dyes because the yarns used to weave the fabrics have already been individually dyed and varying combinations of colors create plaids, stripes, and tweeds. Plaids and stripes can be printed onto base cloths but these should not be confused with actual yarns dyes in which the design is woven in. Other woven-in designs include jacquards and dobbys which require more complicated loom controls than basic weaves.

Knitted fabrics come in various weights determined by the density and twist of the yarns. Knits are almost always part of a sportswear group. They are also widely used in childrenswear, active sport, menswear, and nearly every other category of design. Sweater knits are classified by fiber, type of stitch, and gauge. Gauge refers to the closeness of the needles used by a knitting machine or the fineness of the cloth. **Denier** refers to yarn thickness and thus to gauge, but it is used more often in the hosiery industry when the knitting is extremely fine. Knits are sold as piece goods for **cut-and-sew** production or garment parts can be manufactured individually and stitched together for a **full-fashioned** sweater. The samples for approval that are sent back to the designer from the knitter are called **knit downs**.

Interesting and unusual fabrics add the spice and excitement to the textile choices that make up a line. These are the pieces with enough visual appeal to sell the group to the buyer. The fabrics are called **novelties**. Novelties can be unusual knits, prints, weaves, or fancy weaves that are then printed. They are an important component of most sportswear groups.

Many manufacturers and product development teams design their own novelty fabrics rather than buying what the mills have to offer. Textiles differentiate the product; they make it special or different from other products in the same category. By designing their own textiles, companies have the assurance that what they are showing for the season is uniquely theirs; that no other company will be using the same print or the same plaid, and in some cases, not even the same weave.

DESIGNING TEXTILES FOR A LINE OR GROUP

A designer who works for a print house or a mill will design a group of fabrics based on a theme. This is called a *collection* (see Plate 17). In a collection, all of the fabrics are not designed to be used together, but rather to be selected from on the basis of the original theme. For example, a textile artist can decide to use an animal theme for children's clothing. The color story will remain constant, but the actual print designs may have images of teddy bears and puppies wearing bandanas and other images of kittens, and so forth. In a coordinated group of fabrics, on the other hand, the designs are all made to be used together. So the puppies wearing bandanas might have an allover print of bandanas as a coordinate and a third coordinate might be a stripe in the same colors to match. Sometimes a designer will create a *coordinated* group of fabric prints to be used together (see Plate 18). At other times, a single print can be chosen from a collection of prints to be used as a novelty item or print for a blouse or shirt in a men's or women's sportswear group. Consideration should always be given to the scale of the print as it relates to the customer and the end use. A tiny floral might create a problem for the women's size market; an oversized geometric print may not work for toddler girls.

PRINTED FABRICS

Without delving deeply into the technology of printing, some basic points should be mentioned. A design for a print is created in seasonal palette colors. The design is then put into repeat, or duplicated in a certain pattern so that when the design is printed it will appear all over the length and width of the cloth without any visible breaks or interruption in the design.

The design can be printed using a number of different processes which use either paper or vinyl film, flatbed screens, rotary screens, or engraved cylinders. Most mass-produced fabrics use cylinders and in this case the designer will send the original design in repeat to the engraver who will create the cylinder. Each color in the design will require its own cylinder. The cylinders will be used for the printing process and a test run will be conducted to determine the accuracy of the engraving and the color match between the original and the sample. This sample is called a *strike-off* and is sent back to the design room for approval. Once color standards for the print are established and the strike-off is accepted, fabric production can begin.

Printing technology has advanced to the point that digital printing, right from the CAD system to a high-end printer, is possible. A designer can see the fabric he or she has designed printed on cloth right in his or her own studio—if the company can afford the Iris or Stork® printer, that is. The cost of these printers is very high and presently unaffordable for smaller manufacturers. Service companies are available that provide high-level printouts for a fee. The output from these high-end printers looks so much like real fabric that at first glance it is difficult to differentiate the real swatch from a paper one. These printers also have the capacity to print onto various types of fabric.

There are hopes that this technology will offer opportunities for full production of textiles rather than just sample yardage within the next decade. If this comes to pass, the entire engraving and/or screen process can be bypassed and the cost of strike-offs from the mill can be eliminated. Even under present circumstances, the number of strike-offs that designers have to request from printers has been greatly reduced because of CAD technology.

When a designer begins working on textile designs, he or she should know something about the printing process that the company will use. For example, the circumference of the roller will determine the vertical repeat; the width of the cylinder will determine the horizontal repeat. The standard size for a rotary screen is 25.25 inches. In flatbed printing, the screens are 30, 32, or 36 inches wide. These specifications become parameters of the design work.

Print design usually begins with a motif. This motif can be a completely abstract group of lines or shapes or a recognizable object such as a flower or a toaster. But the motif is the subject of the entire textile design and is repeated, added to, or subtracted from until either a single fabric or an entire group of fabrics is created. CAD technology makes this part of the process more expansive and creative than ever before, because so many more varieties of a motif can be experimented with quickly. The number of design possibilities and varieties that a designer can come up with during a work week is exponential compared with pre-CAD times.

The motif that a designer chooses will be based on the type of print that the end product will become. The type of print is dictated by the perceived needs of customers and the end use of the product. Print types include:

1. *Traditional*—the classics such as paisleys, calicoes, Liberty prints, and foulards
2. *Florals*—botanical images, both realistic and stylized
3. *Conversational*—any recognizable image: objects, characters, animals, etc.
4. *Abstract*—made of geometric forms or paint splashes or other nonrealistic arrangements of line and color. These arrangements can also be geometrically organized into stripes, plaids, dots, etc.
5. *Historical*—related to other cultures and time periods and may be inspired by research of other time periods, cultures, and surface design processes
6. *Stripes, plaids, and weave imitations or textures*—designs to be printed. This should not be confused with woven-in or knitted plaids, stripes, and textures

Once a type of print is decided on and a motif developed, the designer has to come up with a layout, or a way the motif is placed or organized on the fabric. The layout includes decisions regarding the type of layout, the amount of coverage and the direction of the layout.

The types of layouts are based on a grid, real or imaginary, and the motif can be placed on the grid in a set pattern or arrangement according to a plan. The repeat shapes can be arranged horizontally or vertically on a square grid, a diamond-shaped grid, or an ogee grid. The individual motifs can be organized in rows or in circles, or may be connected to one another in a certain way. The motif can be flipped, mirrored, or rotated any number of degrees.

A **half drop** is a print in which a horizontal or vertical row of repeated motifs is established. The next row of motifs is placed half the measurement of the motif down from the original. A **quarter drop** repeat is similar, but the second row only drops one-fourth of the distance down from the first. Sometimes drop patterns are called brick layouts, a term which makes the arrangement easier to visualize.

Motifs can also be arranged in a random way which appears to have no definite plan (although every repeat has to be planned or it will not repeat). The motif can be arranged as a stripe or even as a border along one edge of the fabric. Sometimes prints are *engineered* to fit a certain size piece of fabric as in the case of scarves and pillowcases. The motifs are also laid onto the fabric in a particular direction (see Plate 19):

1. *One-way*. All the motifs are placed in the same direction. The finished fabric has to be cut with the pattern pieces all going in one direction (like napped fabric).
2. *Two-way*. The motifs are flipped either horizontally or vertically so the fabric can be used in both directions.

3. *Four-way.* The motif is flipped vertically and mirrored horizontally so the fabric can be used in both directions.
4. *Tossed.* The motif looks as if it has not been arranged in any particular direction.

The designer will also be concerned with how much open space or air is left among the individual motifs, or how tightly packed they are. He or she will determine how much coverage the print will encompass—whether it is a tight arrangement or a more open, airy one.

Along with the motif, a designer should consider the ground the motif rests on. Will it be a solid color? Will another arrangement of the same motif or coordinated motifs serve as the ground? Perhaps a textural design should be part of the ground, or the texture could appear as an overlay on the arranged motifs. The variety and possibility are boundless.

Very often, the original print design will serve as the starting point for the rest of the coordinated group. For example, in a floral, the leaf can be isolated from the flower and a fabric can be created that incorporates just the leaf as an allover pattern. Next, a third coordinate can be created by changing the scale of the original flower and making it larger or smaller to create a new repeat and additional fabrics. Stripes, plaids, and textures can be generated to serve as a ground and the motif of the flower or the leaf can be placed over the ground for another new fabric. Plate 20 shows a stripe design in two colorways that will be coordinated with the cowboy print shown in Plate 19.

The next step is to establish the colorways for the print. Usually a print will contain approximately six to eight colors (for mass production) and then there will be various arrangements of the colors to create the colorways. Three to four colorways of the same print are usually offered. Since it requires a different screen or roller for each color, the more colors a print contains, the more expensive it will be to produce. In heat transfer printing, the number of colors used in a design is unlimited.

Designers use various methods to establish colorways. Industry-specific CAD systems have the capacity to show the designer all of the possible combinations of colors within a given palette for each particular print. The computer creates the colorways on the screen one at a time and the designer can simply edit them, saving those that are most appealing for a further edit. This saves the time required to substitute a color at a time in the original print, creating all possible new combinations.

The designer working with a computer can also use traditional methods used by textile designers. The following is a brief description of the manual methods for establishing colorways. The term used in the industry for establishing colorways is **pitching**. Pitching a color means to plot the original colors on a chart and fill in the new colors based on specified movements around the color wheel.

Initially, the designer needs to know whether the new color-ways should contain the same intensity and brightness as the original. This is called **weighing in**. If the new colorways maintain the same relationship among colors in terms of their value and chroma, the colors are said to "weigh in." Normally, in apparel design, this is an optimum feature so that the overall mood of the fabrics remains constant.

When a designer pitches a set of colors, the colors in the original print are plotted along the edge of a circle that is labeled red, orange, yellow, green, blue, and violet along the circumference in their proper positions on the color wheel. The color that dominates should be the first one plotted and the others are plotted in descending order of importance. The circle is then replotted for each new colorway. If there is only one other colorway, the circle is divided in half. The first original color moves halfway around the circle in the new colorway. The second original color moves halfway around the circle to become the second color in the new colorway, and so on with each color.

If the designer is working on two new colorways from the original, the circle is divided into thirds and each color moves two-thirds of the way around the circle (clockwise) for each new color in each colorway. The colors can be graphed by name on a chart or by color tab, which is a small splotch of the color rendered in paint or by the computer. The colors can be identified by PAN-TONE TEXTILE Color System® numbers or another color-matching system.

Once the manual method is understood, it can be adapted to the color wheel found in most commercial paint programs. Of course, many designers select their colors more intuitively than this process describes. Even if the approach is used, alterations and adjustments are still necessary.

USING A SCANNER

Many textile designers who work on CAD systems have learned to use a scanner as an important tool in their work. Scanners are available in color and in black and white, but color is essential for commercial use. A scanner will allow an image from a magazine, a photograph, or a piece of fabric to be processed so that it appears on the computer screen. From this point, the designer can manipulate the image in limitless ways. Sometimes, found objects such as pebbles or paper clips are laid on the scanning bed and input to generate design ideas.

Scanning an image for use as a motif or a textile pattern takes some experience with the software that is running the scan and an understanding of memory problems associated with the procedure. A black-and-white line drawing takes up the least amount of memory on a disk or hard drive. Sometimes it is useful to scan in a design or motif in black and white or grey scale and then add color once it has been imported into a paint program.

Scanning in a full-color image can take up a vast amount of memory; very often too much to fit on a high-density disk. Since the scanner operates by picking up different levels and intensities of light, a five-color piece of fabric that is being scanned in can be read by the scanner to contain thousands of colors. This is because of the reflection of light from the surface texture of the fabric. In terms of the memory allocations in most standard computers, a scan with thousands of colors is a large and unmanageable document. First, the designer should scan in the smallest possible portion of the image, so that as little memory as possible is taken up on the disk or hard drive.

Next, the number of colors in the image has to be reduced to the lowest possible number while still maintaining the integrity of the design. Most graphics programs have the capacity to do this color reduction, but it takes some time and experience to accomplish it well. Next, the designer will "clean up" the image. This removes extraneous pixels of color that don't belong in the design, and tightens up the appearance of the edges and outlines of the components of the image or the motif. Then comes the problem of color matching, which was discussed in Chapter 5. It can take some time to match what is on the screen with the original. Once the design is printed onto paper (or fabric, if the technology is available), colors have to be matched again because what is seen on the screen is rarely what the printer will produce.

Note that when scanning in a design, there will be less difficulty in cleaning and color reduction if the image to be scanned is a painting rather than a fabric swatch. Of course, this is not always a possibility. The scan must be saved in a file format that is readable by the software that will be used to manipulate the image. **TIFF** is the standard file format accepted by the apparel industry, but PICT or PCX is also readable by most paint programs.

Once the designer has isolated the motif and recolored it, the functions offered by the software program can be used to create the repeat. Sometimes, a few different motifs can be developed from a single scan and used to create a coordinated group of fabrics. A scan composed of a certain group of colors can be completely recolored to match the prespecified seasonal palette.

Print design is very simple to simulate using commercial paint and graphics programs. Many software packages have a tiling component which allows the original motif to be picked up and repeated over and over again. Half-drops can be made by using measuring tools to lay one motif down, measure half the distance of the motif horizontally and vertically, and then place another motif down at that point. Some software offers an "offset" feature that can create a half drop or quarter drop. In industry-specific CAD systems, the designer can assign a weave to the print; that is, the print can be done on a twill, a plain weave, a satin weave, and so on, and the texture created by the weave can be visualized.

Industry-specific knitwear programs can take a print and create stitches on the fabric or on a knitting graph that the knitting machine or hand knitter can follow.

This texturized look can be simulated in paint and graphics programs for purposes of visualization. Various weave or knit textures can be scanned into the computer and layered over or under the prints. A tablet can be attached to the computer and the stylus can be scraped over various textures of paper or board and this can be saved as a texture to be used in combination with a print. CD ROMs are available with stored textures and fabrics that can be used in combination with prints or as a way to give depth and texture to solid fabrics.

COMPUTERIZED PATTERN GENERATION

A number of software programs are on the market that automatically generate patterns based on mathematical formulas (see Plates 21 and 22). The designer will start the system by drawing an initial motif or even a squiggle and the software will take over and generate continuous patterns based on the input. Although this concept has been in existence for many years, textile designers are now using it to capture weaves and patterns. The designer can stop the generation at any point and isolate the image on the screen at that point and manipulate it or import it into another program.

Photo credit: Laura Satori

Interview with
Jhane Barnes
Designer, Jhane Barnes, Inc.

R.W.C.: When did you start using computers to design your fabrics?

Barnes: I started out with an Atari in the early 80s, using cheap dot-matrix printers and little Atari game computers and printing out in black and white to check the weave. I used colored pencils to color in the designs and then eventually wove them on a hand loom (which was also controlled by the Atari). Because the computer was taking care of the details of operating the loom, I could concentrate more on the design and less on the details of the weave. As a result, my designs became more complex, with longer repeats and more complex color arrangements.

R.W.C.: Was your original training in weaving?

Barnes: No, actually my early training was in fashion design concentrating on patternmaking and construction. As I was getting my business started, I could not find fabric I liked. I was a menswear designer, and the men's fabrics were all boring and women's fabrics were not suitable because of looser constructions. I bought a loom and taught myself how to weave using books. Then in 1988 I switched from the Atari to the Mac and it was, "Wow! What a difference."

Back then, I was using basic UltraPaint™ and Superpaint® software on the Mac. Once I had my design in Superpaint®, I would put in the weaves (structures) to create professional (loom-ready) fabrics. I bought software from AVL to help me. I have their jacquard program, their dobby software . . . actually, I have everything of theirs! The AVL system was part of the professional part of my software, but in the early development of their software, you couldn't do anything without Superpaint®, UltraPaint™, or Pixelpaint®. I've also looked at more expensive systems and they're really not for me, because I constantly buy new software, and to be boxed into using one very expensive system that only does one thing doesn't make any sense.

R.W.C.: It sounds like the computer has become a very important design tool for you.

Barnes: As you learn to use the computer, you learn how to design differently. I think it has taught me to be a better designer, to be more organized, and to really think about my design ahead of time. People may say the computer is doing it for you, that it is limiting. That's wrong. It's the other way around. It has absolutely made me a better designer.

R.W.C.: In what new ways have you used the computer recently?

Barnes: In the past few years, I've graduated to the next step by using mathematics software. Everyone thinks I'm crazy, but that's fine. I use mathematics to create patterns.

Let's compare this to how I used to work. In the past, I would go to Superpaint® to do the design in black and white and then I would go into Pixelpaint® to do the colors and then back to Superpaint® for the corrections. Then maybe I would go to Multicolor for the output and repeat, moving into the jacquard program to put the design in weaves. Sometimes I would use three, four, or even five programs for one fabric.

Now, with mathematical programs, I add another step. I use the mathematical program for the inspiration, then use other programs to make the design into the final fabric. The difference is instead of using a pen or my mouse to draw something from scratch, the computer is generating patterns through algorithms. Of course, while it's true the computer is generating the patterns, the idea still comes from me. That's the major difference from my past work. I have two mathematicians that worked with me in Syracuse, New York. We worked via modem and telephone. I tell them the constraints of the loom and how I want to thread the loom. I have ideas I express visually, but now I can think of them in mathematical terms. I couldn't do that in the beginning, but now I understand how they interpret my visual information into mathematics, and so we communicate very well.

Is the computer automatically generating the design? Yes it is, but the idea came from me and I am just as creative as when I used my pencil. The exciting part is graduating to another step and not just thinking of the mouse and screen as though they were merely pen and paper. Now I've gone even further, thinking about the way algorithms control the computer and how I can have them automatically develop patterns for me. Every season I have to keep thinking of new ideas to give to my mathematicians to generate new groups of patterns.

R.W.C.: Now, when you come up with an image on the screen based on the algorithms, do you select a portion that you like?

Barnes: Yes, you have to be very alert. It's just as if you're sitting down to play a piano. You'd better be up for it, you'd better be ready, because if you make any mistakes, you'll have to start over. The software is moving so fast your brain has to be right there with it. If you're not rested, you're going to get junk; if you're not ready, you're going to get junk. It's really quite a different way of designing. It's like a video game and you have to be good at it.

R.W.C.:   So, by keeping up with it, does it mean freezing it at the right time?

Barnes: Well, freezing it at the right time but you also have to know exactly what you're looking for. So you have to have a good sense of design. And you are not working with just a single parameter. You've got the threading and the tie-up and the treadling, three different choices you can make with software. So you might say, "Oh, that's a good threading but I'm not thrilled with the tie-up, let me freeze this, change the tie-up, and now the treadling. Let me combine another scheme with this." So there are lots of design decisions I have to make, though the software is very smart.

R.W.C.:   Do you use off-the-shelf mathematical programs?

Barnes: There are many kinds of mathematical software that I use. I'm using fractal programs and symmetry programs. A fractal is infinite, so it keeps on repeating everywhere. You have to know the level at which to freeze it but that's only one little issue. The big problem is that you've got this crazy, psychedelic image and now you've got to make it into a fabric. So I capture from the screen and go into Color'In and try to get a good repeat. That could take hours or days. Fractals give you similar objects which all have a similar feel to them even though the patterns are infinite. I designed several seasons using a $60 off-the-shelf program. That is amazing when you think of it!

R.W.C.:   It sounds like there's some danger involved with a nondiscriminating user of the program, someone who could be happy with anything that shows up on the screen because the technology is so exciting.

Barnes: That's true with computers in general. You see work done by people who have just gotten their computer and they're thrilled with the fact that it prints out and they're not looking at the fact that what they've printed out is ugly. I can always tell how long somebody has been working on the computer because the longer you're on it, the more discriminating you are. You tend to throw things away more easily than you did before because you develop the pattern more quickly than you did by hand. With experience you can become more prolific, but you have to be more discriminating. I think the good thing about the computer is it can bring out the creativity in people who may have thought they didn't have any. They might know what good design is, but they can't draw it with their hands.

For example, I can't sketch silhouettes very well. I never could. I totally had to overachieve when I was in school. I had to draw it ten times to get it right. Now I do all my sketches in Canvas, and they're more professional looking. Does that mean that the person who can draw it by hand more effortlessly is a better artist than I am? Yes, as an illustrator, but not as a designer because the final result is the most important thing. I feel the same way about textile designs. Just because you can't draw a perfect flower doesn't mean that you're any less of a designer. It's the final result that counts and you can find another way to get that flower. There are all these little quickie programs out there now that can tile anything you want, but after a while you can recognize if someone did not spend long on that pattern. The design always reflects the time and effort that went into creating it.

R.W.C.: Who's in your league in terms of using the computer for textile design?

Barnes: Right now, many designers are using the computer to scan in things that they see in a magazine, or they scan existing fabric in and change it. We don't even have a scanner (well, actually we do, I keep forgetting that our color printer is a scanner too, but we never use it as a scanner). We create everything from scratch on the computer, and there's a huge difference in the product. I don't think there are too many other fabric designers who work from scratch but there might be design studios that do. I hope they do.

R.W.C.: In a sense, then, you are a pioneer in the textile design area because you do all of your work on screen and use inexpensive software rather than the high-end industrial systems.

Barnes: Yes. I imagine people out there are going to think there's something wrong with me using all these cheap software programs when I could be using ones that cost more money, but I see it the other way. Why are they spending so much money when all software does is the technical end? It doesn't help you in being creative. It's not inspiring, it's just helping you do the technical parts. So, what happens? You have designers working and they give their files to the technical person who's using the expensive program to put it in repeat and then, who's the designer? The designer is not even going to be able to take the design all the way to the end, because the technical person is going to change frequently to make it squish into the repeat for the loom. That's a shame. If I were the designer, I would have wanted to control it from start to finish. We do.

R.W.C.: Then your finished design work is mill ready?

Barnes: My mills are thrilled that what I give them is so exact that they can directly interpret it. Most often, they're given hand paintings with too many colors. When they scan it in, they have to spend hours reducing the colors, but with my printouts, they're exactly the right repeat to fit on their looms.

R.W.C.: So what about the future? What programs do you see designers using in the coming years?

Barnes: Textile and graphic software are going to be inexpensive and everybody is going to have a large selection of programs to choose from. The hard part will be knowing what each program does. This is something we do here already. I may go from Superpaint® to Ultrapaint® to Pixelpaint® back to Artworks because there are one or two things I like that they didn't put in the other programs. You have to be up on it, you have to be constantly reading. I consider all that fun and I find it is inspirational.

I think plug-ins are going to be part of the future. A plug-in can be made easily and inexpensively, so why write a whole Photoshop®, if all that's needed is to write this little thing that makes repeats? I think that's going to be the future of software. Whoever has bought and is still buying those big expensive programs are going to be using them as they are now, technically, and they're going to find their design room is clamoring to get something a little more fun and easy to use.

Stripes

Simple stripes can be created using a drawing program to measure distances between lines and filling with palette colors. These lines can be ruler straight or have more of a painterly, hand-drawn, wavy quality depending on the designer's goal. Of course, the width of the stripes can vary and the arrangement of colors can be experimented with. Motifs can be resized or scaled down and laid out in a striped arrangement as well.

Woven-In Designs

It is possible to simulate a woven-in design without an industry-specific program. Brush transparencies and tints can be used to simulate the new colors created at the intersections of the warp and weft threads. Gradient fills can also be used for interesting color changes. Pattern fills and pattern edit functions can offer texture and interesting effects. Plug-ins are commercially available for stripe and plaid generation. **Weave diagrams** and **peg plans** are complicated and difficult to accomplish using off-the-shelf programs, but simulations allow for adequate visualization.

Patterns in Knitting

When designers create patterns for knits, a graph is made showing the placement of each yarn color. This can be simulated by commercial programs by creating an on-screen grid that relates to the gauge of the knit. A sample of the yarn is knitted into a swatch and measured to determine gauge. Then a grid can be generated on screen to reflect the number of stitches per inch in each direction. Each block is then filled in with color. If the program has a layering function, the grid can be laid over the pattern. Each block or cell should only show one color, so the designer will have to manually determine which color to fill the block with when two colors appear.

STUDY QUESTIONS AND PROBLEMS

1. Use the menswear palette created in Chapter 5. Create a plaid for your male customer with a woven or textural effect. (Remember the images of your customer established in the previous chapters.) Display the grid and rulers and determine the vertical and horizontal elements for the composition. Use the gradient, fountain and texture fills to vary the application of the color. If your program has a tint or transparency function, you can automatically create the new colors at the intersections of warp and weft colors. When the pattern is established, use the duplicate or cut, copy, and paste commands to fill the screen. Save your new plaid fabric.

2. Create a two-color, one-way layout for shirting fabric for your male customer. Use the pattern edit functions or the pattern dialogue box to change one of the existing patterns. Place the motif in repeat with the edit commands, by duplicating or using the offset functions, if available.

3. Use your childrenswear palette and design a four- to six-color motif up to 2 inches by 2 inches. If you have a scanner, you may scan in a motif using a piece of artwork, a found object, or a black-and-white photograph. Save it as a PICT, PCX, or TIFF file. Recolor it using the childrenswear palette but maintain the 2-inch by 2-inch dimensions. Using this single motif, create a coordinated group of fabrics for your customer which includes the following layouts: a two-way square repeat, a four-way, half drop repeat, and a tossed repeat. Use the rulers and grid options, the duplicate, cut, copy, paste, rotate, stretch, and skew commands.

4. Use the tossed pattern created in problem 3 and scale your motif up to create a larger design. Add or reduce the negative space, if necessary. Using the CMYK, RGB, or PANTONE Color System numbers that you recorded in the palette generated in Chapter 5, substitute colors and create a new colorway. Keep the "mood" of the original design as well as the pitch and weight of the colors. Scale the motif down and repeat the project, creating a third colorway.

5. Scale your motif up so that it fills the screen. Create a grid on your screen that is five cells wide by four cells long per inch. Overlay the grid on the motif to simulate a knit graph. Make sure each cell has only one color showing.

Chapter 7

Silhouette

According to Mary Brooks Picken, author of the indispensable *Fashion Dictionary*, a silhouette is "the outline or contour of a costume. The 'new silhouette' at the beginning of any season, means the general contour in fashion at the time, especially at the waistline, skirt length, shoulder width, etc., differ(ent) from those of the previous season."[22] Silhouette is the overall shape of the design as it appears on the body.

Historically, silhouette has been established by designers who set a trend for a particular season or time period. Clothing worn during certain time periods often has a very strong identity with a particular silhouette. Examples of time-period silhouettes include the raised empire waistline worn during the Napoleonic Empire period, which drew attention to décolletage; the bustle skirt at the end of the nineteenth century, which emphasized the derriere; and the Gibson Girl silhouette in the early twentieth century, which focused on the full, rounded bosom.

Later, Paul Poiret and then Jean Patou liberated women from the restrictive silhouettes of the time and gave birth to the idea of more comfort in dressing. Poiret lowered the waistline to the hips, Patou raised it below the breasts, and in the 1920s, it was done away with altogether and the chemise dress was originated. Coco Chanel boldly designed trousers for women and included knitted jerseys in her work; women everywhere began to require comfort and function in clothing. Elsa Schiapparelli widened shoulders and this moved into the broad-shouldered suits worn during the 1940s when women joined the professional workforce. This direction extended to Hollywood's glamour period led by the designer Adrian.

Then came Christian Dior with his "New Look," a cinched waist, small rounded shoulders, and a full, calf length skirt. Claire McCardell pioneered American sportswear looks and separates dressing and later, in the 1960s and 1970s, the mini and the hip hugger, the A-line dress, and the pants suit became the mode.

This brief, historical overview shows silhouette changes over time. The bustle, the empire waistline, the Gibson Girl, and the mini length each was a shape change that focused on a particular part of the anatomy. When Patou brought the chemise into vogue and Dior the "New Look," the radical silhouette change was a result of that particular designer's approach to fashion for a particular season—his personal and somewhat dramatic statement.

Another important influence in the determination of silhouette is lifestyle or the designer's feeling about the way clothes should be designed based on a way of living. Chanel certainly approached her work with a lifestyle attitude and much later, during the 1980s, Ralph Lauren revolutionized the fashion industry with the same concept: that clothes should be designed to reflect a certain status or position in life. Aside from being beautiful, this clothing was required to function within the parameters of that lifestyle; in other words, to "work" for the wearer in terms of comfort and practicality as well as status. Today, many designers, manufacturers, and retailers create apparel with a lifestyle point of view—the Gap, J. Crew, Benneton, Tommy Hilfiger, Abercrombie & Fitch, and Banana Republic, just to name a few.

HOW MUCH CHANGE IS CHANGE?

The advent of each new season sends designers scrambling for a new approach to their lines. Some designers such as Calvin Klein and Giorgio Armani have taken a classic view of clothing. Classics are styles that withstand time. This is opposed to the notion of a trend or fad in which clothes last for a season or two and then disappear. A Chesterfield coat is an example of a classic style; thigh-high stockings are an example of a fad in clothing that only lasted for a season or two. Consider the empire waistline mentioned previously. It is a look that goes back in history nearly two hundred years. In childrenswear, the empire waistline is consistently used. It is more than a classic; it is a staple silhouette that is always part of a line. This is because this silhouette is so flattering to the physique of a young girl that it is unaffected by fad or trend.

In women's clothing, however, we have seen the empire waistline come and go during our own lifetimes. In this case, the classic silhouette is popular for a period of time, it recedes and then returns. The empire was not very popular during the 1950s, but very important during the 1960s and 1970s. There was an ebb in the next decade even though it never disappeared entirely. It is presently seen again in many collections. Even the classics move in and out of popularity.

For the most part, designers really don't create anything completely new. Textile science and technology periodically invent new fibers that become new fabrics and these are used by designers. Essentially, fashion continually recombines old elements in novel and creative ways. Designers gain new perspectives on old proportions and reinvent combinations of shapes and details that existed before. Silhouettes are repetitious and cyclical and apparel designers are continually challenged to see the old in a new and exciting way.

Innovation is most often based on using old resources in a new way, or coming up with a new perspective on something as timeless as clothing. Donna Karan's popularization of the body suit is an example of what was a new perspective in dressing. Her idea was that the body suit could become the foundation for many other pieces to be worn and interchanged during a busy woman's workday. The concept was so well received that it became the impetus for a new trend at many market levels.

Occasionally, fashion change is revolutionary—for instance, the idea of throwing away restrictive undergarments during the 1920s and again during the 1960s. Powerful changes in fashion can be brought about by strong cultural and social change. In general, however, fashion is a continuous cycle of new attitudes and approaches toward how we dress ourselves fed by a need for clothes that function well within our lifestyles. Perhaps most importantly, fashion has the capacity to provide us with a sense of beauty and well being.

Fashion Cycles

Fashion operates in cycles; even classics have their time-based parameters of popularity, depending on the market. In all cases of new design development, there is a period in which the new direction is presented to the public. This is the introduction phase and the trendsetters or those who are at the forefront of the fashion scene wear the new trends in color and silhouette for the sake of being fashionable.

The trendsetters set an example for the public and the new fashion increases in popularity and it is worn by more and more people. This is the period of increase. As the fashion becomes integrated into the marketplace at every level and every price point, it reaches its peak, it declines, and is finally rejected. Time passes and the silhouette or idea starts to feel right again to a designer somewhere. He or she reinterprets it in a new way, the style recurs, and the fashion cycle begins again. Sometimes this reinterpretation comes right at the heels of the previous cycle; other times, it takes a long time to recur. Figure 7–1 offers a graphic representation of these cycles.

Designers at haute couture and couture levels often use their studios as testing grounds for new design ideas. They experiment with fabric directly on a body to originate new ways of draping and new ways of thinking about silhouette. They have the latitude to take risks since their clothes have limited production runs. They are designing for a very high status, wealthy client or sim-

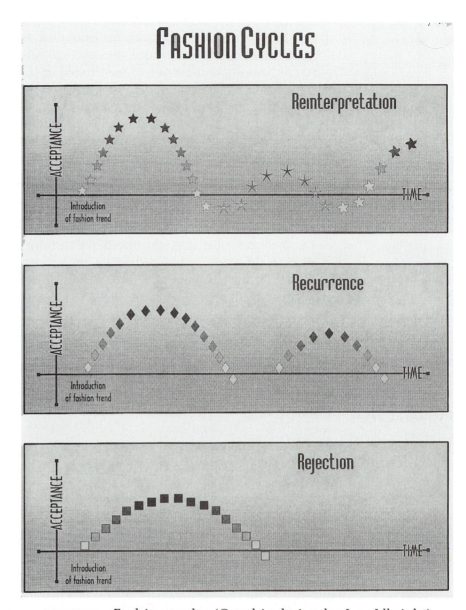

Figure 7–1   Fashion cycles (Graphic design by Lee Albright)

ply for the runway where experimental silhouettes often set the direction for the other price levels of the marketplace.

At the designer level, silhouette often remains very classic. Some response to new trends occurs, but very often the fabrication and color control the mood and direction at this price point. The designer customer wants quality in fabrication and construction and endurance in the investment. Enduring style is synonymous with classic style.

Mass market apparel design does not operate at the introductory phase of the acceptance cycle, but rather, at the middle levels of increase, peak, and decline. The changes presented each season are not as radical or trendsetting as in the introductory phase. Currently, merchandisers in the mass market are extremely careful about which silhouettes they include in a line and take few risks. They use tried-and-true silhouettes, or *bodies,* as they are referred to in the industry, and repeat the successful styles season after season. Color and fabric change, but the profitable silhouette is carried. In the mass segment of the industry, change is gradual. It is often fueled by couture and designer levels or by street fashion and youth movements.

UNDERSTANDING SHAPE

Silhouette is the overall shape of the garment as it appears on the body. Silhouette can also be understood in terms of the distance from the body that the fabric maintains. A body-hugging silhouette acts as a second skin. The natural silhouette skims the natural body shape, and the moderate silhouette, which may have some padding in the shoulders or fullness in the fabric that camouflages the natural body, creates a new shape of its own. Extreme silhouettes change, distort, or eliminate the sense of all or part of the body underneath the clothing. There can be extensive control and redefinition of the figure underneath the clothes, as in a padded corset. There can also be distance from the body, as in extremely broad shoulders, oversized trousers, or a full, draped skirt.

Historians, customers, and designers have studied and classified silhouette based on geometric shapes:

1. The *body-hugging* shape is tightly fitted, close to the body or stretching around it and controlling it. Examples are body suits, leggings, and swimsuits (see Figure 7–2a).

2. The *hourglass* shape is widest at the shoulder and hip with a narrow, pinched waist (see Figure 7–2b). The shoulders and hips can be natural or exaggerated. Examples are the shirt waist dress, a "fit and flare" dress, a suit, or a coat.

3. The *pencil or tubular* shape is long, thin, and fluid from top to bottom (see Figure 7–2c). This is normally a natural or moderate silhouette. A chemise dress, Chanel cardigan jacket, and slim skirt are examples of tubular silhouettes. Many coats are based on a tubular shape.

4. The *inverted triangle* shape is usually exaggerated with broad shoulders that taper to a narrow hem (see Figure 7–2d). Off-the-shoulder designs or huge, oversized sleeves are examples of inverted triangle shapes if the lower part of the garment is kept narrow.

5. The *triangle or pyramid* shape is narrow at the shoulder and full at the hemline (see Figure 7–2e). The A-line dress is a moderate example of the triangle. A tunic with a very full, draped

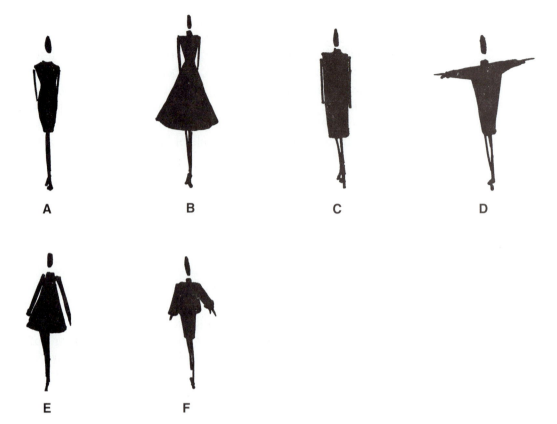

A   B   C   D

E   F

Figure 7–2   Silhouettes (Illustrations by Roberta Hochberger Gruber)

skirt is an example of a more exaggerated silhouette. A tent dress or coat is a triangle shape that can be moderate or exaggerated.

6. The *blouson* shape refers to a large rectangular or rounded shape on the top portion of the body. The bottom may be narrow or flared (see Figure 7–2f).

Fabric Selection and Silhouette

The type of fabric that a designer chooses is important to achieving success in the intended silhouette. If a body-hugging silhouette is desired, stretch fabrics that mold to the body are a good choice. If an extreme silhouette is what the designer is after, the fabric has to have a good deal of stiffness or body to maintain the design. In extreme silhouettes, lots of fabric volume is usually necessary as are various underpinnings such as padding, stiffeners, boning, and wiring which hold the fabric in the desired position.

Decisions about silhouette should not be made until the designer has worked with the actual fabric. The cloth should be draped on a form or body to make sure that the fabric will do what the designer intends it to. Fabric is the medium of fashion, not paper and pencil or even a computer. The latter are simply the tools used to communicate information about the garment.

Proportion

Proportion is determined by dividing the length of the body into horizontal lines in order to establish relationships among the parts. These lines are the shoulder, the waist, and the hem (see Figure 7–3). In the case of separates, more than one hemline horizontal may have to relate to the other horizontals. The lines become shapes when they are given a controlled length and connected to each other. For example, the breadth of the shoulder is decided on and then the shoulder points are connected to the breadth of the waist or the hem.

The next step is to control the relationships of the shapes to one another. The shape created from the shoulder to the waist in a short jacket must relate proportionally to the shape created by the horizontal at the waist connected to the horizontal at the hem in a skirt or pants. The proportions of the various parts always have to be seen in relationship to the entire length of the body. A successful proportioning of the parts of a garment or an outfit must enhance the appearance of the person wearing the clothes and be visually pleasing.

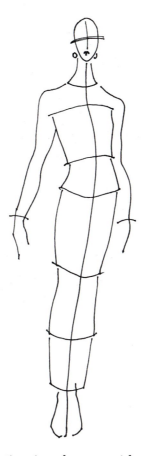

Figure 7–3 Good proportion involves consideration of related shapes as they appear on the body (Illustration by Roberta Hochberger Gruber)

Proportion is sometimes broken down into a formula based on the overall number of head lengths in a body by a rule in fine art known as the "golden mean." While this is a rather foolproof method for establishing proportion, a designer with a good eye will be able to fine-tune proportion instinctively. He or she will be able to adjust the length of individual layers of ruffles in a skirt visually as well as determine the right jacket length to go well with a skirt length. Following this instinct will allow the designer to push the parameters of proportion that a rule-based mode of design will not allow.

Like silhouette, proportion changes as fashion changes. A short, waist-length jacket with a calf-length dirndl skirt is a proportion that may not feel right for this period of time; a short, straight skirt with a thigh-length fitted jacket is an acceptable proportion in today's marketplace. A designer looks carefully at the relationship of the lengths and shapes of pieces when they are worn together. Sometimes, a designer will reduce the sweep of the skirt by a few inches to make a jacket proportion that will work with the skirt. Or perhaps lengthening the skirt by just half an inch will make the proportion of the jacket work with the skirt. It goes without saying that the customer always wants to look his or her best and this usually means as tall and thin as possible. A designer's control over color, fabrication, silhouette, proportion, and line have everything to do with successfully meeting the needs of the customer.

Line

The organization of the visual and structural components of a garment is referred to as the line (see Figure 7–4). Silhouette is the overall shape of the garment, usually read by the edges; but line is created by the elements within the interior of the silhouette such as seams, trimmings, and details. For example, two vertical seams originating at the shoulder or armhole and going over the bust line to the hem of the garment is a princess line. These two lines can be shaped in a variety of ways and their relationship to each other can give the garment a homemade, dowdy look, or the lines can go over the body in a provocative, sexy way. Most of the time, line is created by structural or fitting elements such as seams or stylized darts and contour lines, but very often trimmings used as embellishments add interest to the garment. The placement of these trimmings is another way to create line and a good designer has to consider their use carefully. Once line is added, the relationship of the resulting panels will determine how thin the wearer will look when she puts the dress on. If the proportion of the center panel is too wide in relationship to the side panels, the person will look broad; if the center panel is too narrow, the person will still look broad because the side panels will call attention to the width of the body.

Overall proportion was defined earlier by the three basic horizontals—shoulder, waist, and hem. But the internal shapes

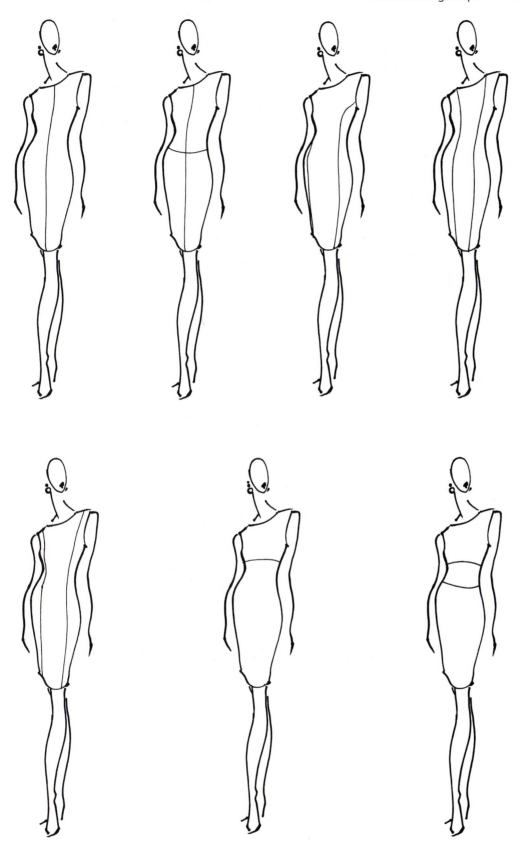

Figure 7–4 Examples of various ways line can be placed within a silhouette (Illustrations by Roberta Hochberger Gruber)

created by line also affect proportion, especially when color is added. In Figure 7–5, the placement of light and dark color help to accent or minimize different parts of the body.

Focal Point

Harmony and balance are the goals a designer strives for when working with silhouette, line, color, proportion, and fabrication. As each new design is scrutinized, the designer should think about where his or her eye rests when looking at the garment. In other words, where is the focal point? If you can isolate the focal point, be sure that it enhances the garment and the person wearing it (see Figure 7–6).

Sometimes it is best not to have a focal point at all but to keep the eye moving. Diagonal lines have this effect. The elements of line, proportion and focal point can be studied in principle, but the best way to truly understand them is by experience. Shop the stores, look at what people are wearing, and try to understand harmony and balance as it exists in real products.

Cut, Fit, and Construction

The most beautiful garment is useless if it does not fit properly. Clothes are made to function on a body and if they are not cut to fit they will not turn a profit. Good fit is something that the wearer feels. Trying on a Giorgio Armani jacket is a good way to experience fit. It should be weightless because it hangs perfectly from the shoulder; it should be comfortable because the armhole is cut well; it shouldn't gape at the neckline or pull across the shoulder blades.

Ease is an important term to consider when describing fit and shape. Ease is the amount of extra fabric allotted for wearing comfort. When a great deal of ease is added to the shape, the garment is called oversized. When there is very little or no ease, the garment is "skin tight."

It is difficult to discuss or assess cut and fit without understanding construction. If a designer truly understands how clothes are made and what techniques and machinery are used to put them together, he or she will produce designs that are realistic. Each design would have clear indications of all structural lines within the garment. If a designer produced a sketch of a jacket with an hourglass silhouette, the sketch would indicate the constructional elements that would make the silhouette possible to realize. Without fit lines in a drawing, the designer's lack of construction awareness is all too obvious. A pair of pants drawn without an indication of the crotch line, or a dress without a zipper or button opening, shows a designer's inexperience. This is not to say that a designer has to know how to make a suit as well as the company's tailor. Familiarity can be gained by studying clothes as well as by making them.

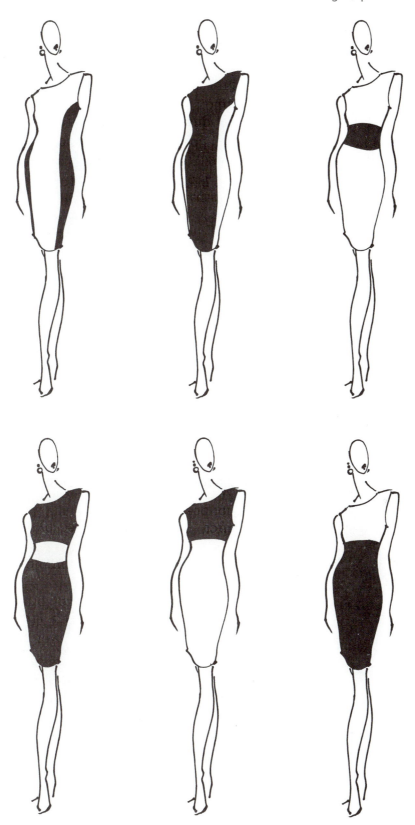

Figure 7–5   Careful placement of color as it relates to line and overall silhouette is important to the success of a design (Illustrations
by Roberta Hochberger Gruber)

Figure 7–6 The focal point of a design should enhance the garment and the body beneath it (Illustration by Roberta Hochberger Gruber)

Coordinating Silhouettes

When a sportswear designer plans a group or a line, individual bodies are designed. The intent, however, is for the individual components to relate to each other and to be interchangeable. The jacket silhouettes have to work with the pants silhouettes and the skirt bodies. The collars of the blouses have to be designed to look good under the jacket necklines; the length of the sweaters have to be proportioned to work with the skirts and the pants. Coordinating silhouettes is a mathematical challenge. Each silhouette has to relate well to the other silhouettes in the group; the more the group can be "mixed and matched," the more options the buyer and ultimately the retail customer will have.

Rendering Silhouette

A rendering or a drawing is a tool for communicating information about a product. Therefore, the nature of the drawing has a great deal to do with the purpose of the communication. Drawings may take the form of illustrations, sketches, or technical specifications.

An illustrator will work in a very stylized way, as an artist does. The images will offer an attitude about the clothes in an artistic way. Shape or silhouette and color will be important elements, but detailed representations of construction lines may be absent or included wistfully. An illustrator will often purposefully distort proportion as part of the stylization. The illustrator's goal is to create a beautiful image usually for purposes of advertising or promoting the product to a customer or particular audience.

A sketch can be an image ranging from a small thumbnail drawn on a napkin in a restaurant to a completely colored, swatched drawing that represents a garment in a line. The amount of information contained in the sketch varies with the habits of the designer doing the sketching and the parameters set by the company the designer is working for. Many designers at the couture or designer levels will create a loose sketch that indicates silhouette and proportion with little reference to construction and detail. This sketch will then be read by an experienced sample hand and patternmaker who will "interpret" the sketch and then the sample will be presented to the designer for modification and approval. Figure 7–7 is a designer's sketch of a jacket; Figure 7–8 shows a technical interpretation of the same garment.

Figure 7–7   Stylized sketch (Courtesy of Calvin Klein, Inc.)

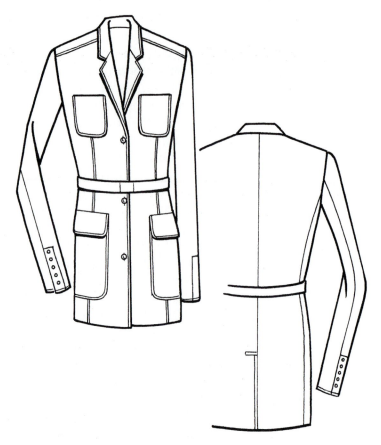

Figure 7–8 CAD-generated technical interpretation of the design (Courtesy of Calvin Klein, Inc.)

Some companies do not have the budget to support the interpretation phase, especially at the mass level, and the designer's sketch has to provide explicit information about construction and detail. This type of sketch can be considered a working drawing; it provides the patternmaking department with enough information that an interpretation is not necessary. But rather, the image itself contains a delineation of stitching lines, details such as pocket and button placement, and so forth.

Once a design idea becomes an accepted body for a line, a sketch for production purposes has to be rendered. This is called a technical drawing or a flat. It communicates all the technical information about a particular body to anyone involved in the production process. It is a realistic, nonstylized drawing that shows the garment in perfect proportion, much like an engineer might create when rendering a machine. The flat is a two-dimensional, flat image of the style and there is usually a back view offered which defines the design details on the back of the garment (see Preproduction Systems, Chapter 3).

The flat drawing is then used in the specifications (spec) sheets that follow the design through production. It is used by the patternmaking department to develop a first pattern then a graded pattern. It is used by production experts to cost the garment and plan the assembly process. Flats may even be used by the merchandising department for inclusion in a product catalogue. The disk included with this book offers many examples of flats and a generic spec sheet.

Computer Rendering of Silhouette

The three types of rendering described in the previous section can all be accomplished using a computer drawing or paint program. Illustrations probably are done least on the computer because it was not until recently that an effort was made by software developers to simulate the artist's drawing experience. Even now, many of the effects that an illustrator can achieve using goache and watercolors are particular to rendering by hand. Conversely, many effects that the computer can achieve are not attainable by hand, which is further support for the computer being seen as a special tool that can offer an experienced illustrator new potential.

The area of photographic imaging has enormous potential for fashion illustrators. Standard computer software such as Adobe Photoshop™ can accomplish many high-level functions that can recreate a drawing or photograph and change its attitude and image entirely.

Presently, computers are used most often to provide detailed drawings of clothing. Drawing software is used to render a flat drawing and entire libraries of designs can be saved on disk. These silhouettes can be recalled and updated or subtly changed from season to season without having to redo the entire sketch. These archived libraries become invaluable company resources and histories.

Photo credit: Laura Satori

Interview with
Heather Johnson
CAD Director, Calvin Klein, Inc.

R.W.C.:   What does your job require of you? How long have you been working at Calvin Klein, Inc.?

Johnson: I have been here for over two years in the position of CAD systems specialist. My initial position consisted of integrating a computer system into the collection design studio. I began by setting up the databases and creating the technical sketches on the computer. I take the designer's fashion illustration and translate it into a technical sketch using the computer. Many of the designers at Calvin Klein, Inc. will probably continue to sketch on paper because they feel that the computer lacks the artistic touch that they develop when sketching by hand. One designer told me that using the stylus on the tablet felt too slippery. I told her that one day technology would compensate for this.

R.W.C.:   How detailed is the illustration you get from the designer?

Johnson: The designer's sketch is far from detailed; it is their interpretation of an expression of design. I understand what they are trying to convey because I work very closely with them. When I am in prototype fittings, I listen to their comments and then back in the design studio I adjust the sketches on my computer. Eventually we will be installing computers in the fitting rooms, so that the designers can correct their specs and instantly alert the rest of the company. After our prototypes are approved, these technical sketches are used for our sample cutting tickets and to create our merchandising books.

R.W.C.:   Did you initiate this process?

Johnson: Yes. In the past, the process of sample cutting tickets was a nightmare. The designers would take a sketch and trace it onto a carbon copy form. If we had one pair of pants planned in six different fabrics, they would trace the same sketch six different times. They would work on the tickets each evening until midnight for three weeks. When I first started here, I produced all the cutting tickets for the collection in two days using the computer. The key to the computer is setting up a majority of the databases ahead of time. After the databases for the sketches, fabrics, colors, mills, and patternmakers are created, producing cutting tickets is a snap. By simply touching on the fabric name, the fabric quality, style number, available colors, and mill name pop up automatically. That's the way computers should work. Later, the showroom personnel said, "Is there a way that you could create our merchandising books on the computer? We would love to use them in the showroom during our market week." My responsibilities keep growing and growing. The more people see what I can do, the more they wonder about the endless possibilities of computers.

R.W.C.: Are you the only one at Calvin Klein, Inc. that has a CAD station now?

Johnson: Presently I am the only CAD user, but this may change in the near future. The designers have discovered how easy it is to see the numerous colorways and repeats that I can create from their stripes, plaids, and prints. I envision a few CAD systems in each design studio.

R.W.C.: How did they describe your job when they hired you?

Johnson: The position required a person who knew how to integrate the computer into a design studio. I was still required to assist the designers, create merchandising boards, draw technical sketches, and work with the patternmakers, but the emphasis was on the computer. The computer was such a new concept that many people were hesitant about how I would successfully computerize the design studio. Within one week I had touched every facet of the collection division with either sample cutting tickets, technical sketches, or merchandising books. The designers were amazed, the patternmakers were thrilled with the accurate computerized information, and the production department could finally analyze the season's work flow ahead of time.

R.W.C.: Do you have a fashion background or a computer background?

Johnson: I was able to create a major that combined the two at the University of Delaware. I started off in fine arts, moved on to advertising, and then discovered a major called interdisciplinary studies. My major allowed me to combine fine arts, fashion, and a concentration in CAD into one degree. The program allowed me to balance all of my interests and excel in my favorite areas. The funny thing is that it was only one class in CAD that drew me toward my present career. When I saw the CAD system I thought that this will satisfy the creative side of my mind and challenge my technical side. The possibilities that CAD technology offers are absolutely endless. I am trying to take CAD to the next plateau by analyzing the work flow within all the different design studios. Even though the designers are excited about CAD, the implementation of the computer has to be analyzed carefully. Now that their artwork can be created in a quarter of the time, how many systems do we really need? The designers love the flexibility that the computer offers them. Before they could only choose a few colorways for the artist to paint, now the possibilities are endless with the implementation of the CAD system.

R.W.C.: So is there a lot of support in this company for your development and the development of the technology?

Johnson: Each time I complete a CAD project, I earn the respect and freedom to develop the CAD department. The most productive area of the CAD department is my teaching/chart-creating center. The center is helping to positively integrate computers into the different divisions. I have set up five computers where the employees from the different divisions come to work on their merchandising charts. Everyone works independently, but if someone has a problem or needs advice, I am right there to help.

R.W.C.: How are the prints designed now?

Johnson: In the past, artwork was sent out, hand painted, and returned within two to four days. Presently, the designers are taking full advantage of my CAD system. Last season, I created 36 stripes, 15 different plaids, and 12 prints in a few days. By turning their designs around in a few hours, we were able to pull together the season's design concept in about one week. I saved them thousands of dollars in painting services.

R.W.C.: Do you foresee a time when this is going to cut down on sample making?

Johnson: Yes. Sometimes fabric is purchased before the sketches are created. With the CAD system, we can lay a color or a print on a photograph and simulate what the design would possibly look like. I did a presentation for Calvin a few weeks ago using this technique so that he could decide the scale of some of our print designs. By seeing a simulation on the computer, he decided on the scale of the print. This process saved the mills from screenprinting three different sizes and the samplemakers from making three new samples.

R.W.C.: What recommendations do you have for students going out into this field?

Johnson: If they would like to enter the fashion industry at a level above and beyond their peers, they need to understand CAD and computers. At least 50 percent of their portfolio should be created using the artistic techniques that the computer offers. I did a rendering on the computer of four figures to show how sensitive a computer's drawing tools could really be. When I opened up my portfolio, the design director and president were amazed at my computerized rendering. They kept touching it and examining it closely—they could not believe a computer had produced it. They briefly glanced over the rest of my portfolio. I think they had made their minds up after seeing my first page. That's what it is all about.

STUDY QUESTIONS AND PROBLEMS *

1. Find the men's, women's and children's flats on the disk. Select a few flats, duplicate them, and practice filling them in using some of the textile designs developed in the problems for Chapter 6. You can use the magic wand tool if it is available to move the flats onto the textile pattern. Be certain that you zoom in on the flat to be certain that there are no spaces along the lines where color might "leak" out. Remember to adjust the scale of the textile design to match the scale of the flat. Use the pencil tool to cover over (erase) any extraneous color, pixel by pixel.

2. Design the silhouettes for a coordinated group of childrenswear for your customer. You may make changes and adjustments to the basic flats on the disk to come up with the new bodies. From your childrenswear palette, choose solid bottom-weight colors to coordinate with the prints designed in Chapter 6, problem 4. Fill the flats with solid color or prints. Try adding texture with the twill example or use the rib texture for a sweater body.

3. Design a group of silhouettes for each of your remaining customers. For the menswear group, create a group of separates for active wear. For the womenswear group, design a career sportswear group for the moderate market.

4. Using the croquis, merchandise each group by combining three garments on a body. You will have to "interpret" your designs or redraw them in a more stylized way so that they can be displayed on the croquis.

5. Using the "Spec Sheet" document, copy and paste each silhouette onto a separate spec sheet and complete the information on each form.

---

*Remember not to permanently alter the images on the disk. Always duplicate the flat or import it into a new document before working with it. Using the "Save As" command will save time.

Chapter **8**

Putting It All Together: Presentation and Graphics

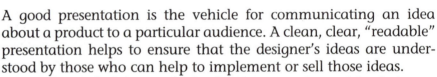

A good presentation is the vehicle for communicating an idea about a product to a particular audience. A clean, clear, "readable" presentation helps to ensure that the designer's ideas are understood by those who can help to implement or sell those ideas.

Fashion designers, textile designers, and graphic designers have all developed visual acumen through academics and experience. The principles of good design are the same for all disciplines. The application of those principles to a specific area of design, such as fashion or graphics, involves combining aesthetics with learned skills and industry methods particular to a specific discipline. A fashion designer will learn how to produce clothing with all the associated technical skills and professional practices; a graphic designer will do the same in his or her discipline.

Can a graphic artist design a dress? Yes. But he or she might not know anything about the feasibility of making and/or selling that dress. By the same token, a fashion designer can create graphic presentations, but he or she is limited by the lack of knowledge in processing and reproducing the graphic design. That lack of knowledge usually shows. Designers have to be careful in crossing over from one discipline to another. It's always a good idea for a fashion designer to enlist the help of a graphic designer when working on an idea or to learn as much as possible about the discipline through study and observation, especially when the work will have to be reproduced by a printing company.

A good presentation will visually relay the designer's intent to the viewer with very little verbal description. When the viewer has to ask for a great deal of explanation, the presentation was probably unclear or confusing. For example, a fashion designer may have to present a line board, which represents all of the silhouettes in a group and the fabrics for each style. The sales staff should immediately be able to understand the colors and fabrics

146

that each style is available in. If they have to ask too many questions, the board isn't clear enough.

When a designer begins to think about creating a presentation, he or she must know the purpose of the presentation and who the audience or viewer will be. Understanding the purpose and audience means knowing exactly what you are trying to communicate and to whom that communication is directed. The audience may be internal or external. An internal audience is made up of members of your design team and employees of other departments within your company. It may also include the retail buyers who are sourcing merchandise for their stores. An external audience consists of the prospective and/or established consumers of the product.

EXTERNAL PRESENTATION MATERIALS

External presentation materials are usually generated by art and graphics departments or the advertising departments within large companies. Sometimes this design work is contracted to outside advertising or graphic design agencies. The presentation materials created by these departments and agencies offer information about the product, but more importantly, they help to establish a company image. An image is the overall impression of a company held by a consumer or buyer. Image directs the consumer to think about a product in a certain way.

A label is an example of how graphic design can create a long-lasting impression to the viewer and an identification with the product. Most of us can see the Calvin Klein, Inc. label or logo in our mind's eye as well as the type style used in the Adidas or Esprit logos. These graphic images establish an attitude toward the product. When we see the Calvin Klein, Inc. label we give certain credence to the product based on the message that the label delivers. We also have certain expectations about the quality of the clothes. When an image is well established, the consumer feels that in some way they have a personal identification with that image.

The wide variety of external presentation material includes:

Logos
Labels
Brochures
Hang tags
Line plans
Swatch cards
Display systems
Catalogues
Videos
Multimedia/CDs

Ad campaign materials
Fashion shows

These graphic materials are used primarily as selling tools. They enhance the buyer's or customer's perception of value. They establish image and are extremely important in "romancing" the product and differentiating it from similar and/or competitive products. A beautiful collection can go unnoticed if it is not presented and promoted in a way that entices the customer; conversely, a seemingly innocuous line of clothes can cause a great stir if the presentation of the clothes is exciting.

INTERNAL PRESENTATION MATERIALS

Internal or in-house presentations include many types of visuals in sheet, catalogue, and board formats. Sometimes designers have to produce a style sheet, which is an information page about a single style in a line (see Figure 8–1). It will show the garment as a flat sketch and/or illustration. The fabric and color choices will be

Road Trip Holiday
Yarn Dye Flannels

Long sleeve woven shirt
Button down collar
Single pocket with Chaps
     pocket tab identification
Self yoke and solid herringbone
     inside collarband

64312 cc 616 barn red   64314 cc 459 midnight   64315 cc 312 moss   64319 cc 070 slate   4

Figure 8–1   A style sheet shows a single silhouette with color and fabric choices (Courtesy of Chaps Ralph Lauren)

indicated. Other documentation such as style number, size range, delivery date, and price will be shown.

The term *board* traditionally was used to mean illustration board, but lightweight foam core is more often used as a presentation medium. Art supply stores have a variety of paper products intended for presentations, including corrugated, prescored, tacky surface, and stand-alone kits. For the most part, internal presentations provide information about mood, theme, color, fabrication, silhouette, and merchandising of the various styles. The types of board presentations used internally, or in-house, include:

> *Color storyboards*—all of the colors that make up the palette usually surrounding a central image from which the hues were "pulled." The color story can be comprehensive, representing all of the colors for a season, or it can be broken down into a particular group, such as colors for men's active wear, women's lingerie, and so on. The colors are represented by yarns, paint chips, swatches, or computer-generated tabs (see Figure 8–2).
>
> *Mood boards*—representations of the feeling of an intended group of garments through a collection of images (see Figure 8–3). Mood boards offer direction to the design team and help to keep a collection of designs consistent and coherent. They also help the merchandisers or sales staff understand the direction of the upcoming line.

Figure 8–2 The "antique" theme of this color storyboard provides the basis for the medium-toned pastel color choices shown by the yarns (Courtesy of Jan Marshall)

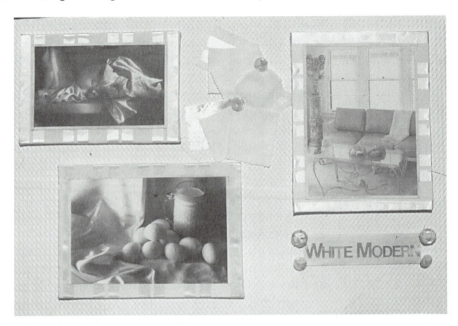

Figure 8–3 This mood board creates a feeling of tonality, transparency, and texture. Spare, clean line is emphasized (Courtesy of Arianne Faunt)

Theme boards—are often interchangeable with mood boards. A theme board offers a visual reference to a topic such as sports or ballet, or craft from various parts of the world (see Plate 23). Examples of themes are baseball, American Indian craft, the art of Andy Warhol, and Pablo Picasso. A theme board highlights the inspirational sources of the potential designs.

Trend boards—show direction for color and silhouette. They provide inspiration and information about the way a line might look without being specific (see Plate 24). A designer can use the images on a trend board to develop initial ideas about shape, proportion, and color.

Fabric boards—represent the textiles that will be used for a line or group. They incorporate the palette established by the color story and show renderings or actual swatches of the fabrics (see Plate 25).

Line boards or line plans—show all of the silhouettes in the group. The images are usually flat and unstylized so that they are very readable by the buyer. They also contain the intended color and fabric for each item in the line (see Plate 27).

Many of these board formats can be combined with each other to create additional types of presentations. A *merchandising board* can show stylized illustrations or sketches of the way the silhouettes and fabrics work together on a body. They help the buyer to imagine the pieces in the line as they are combined with one another.

A company that produces knitted garments may create a *yarn board,* which will showcase new yarns with color choices for each yarn type (see Plate 26). A *sweater board* will contain yarns representing the colors that the sweaters are available in. It will include an illustration or stylized sketch of the finished sweater and a technical drawing or graph of the stitches that make up the pattern.

It is important to note that each company organizes and stylizes its presentations according to its own particular system. A theme board in one company may include illustrations of a silhouette, while in another company, silhouette is kept completely separate.

Sometimes, the graphics department will do internal work as well as external. In some companies, the GAP, for example, the graphics department will help generate the textile designs. On the other hand, in companies such as Hartstrings, the design department will generate the product catalogue (Plate 27). So the divisions described here are flexible. Formats for each type of presentation vary, too, but the ultimate goal is always the same: clear, visually exciting communication.

PLANNING A PRESENTATION

Graphic design involves creating visually pleasing and readable arrangements of image and text on a page. The end goal is to have this composition reproduced using professional printing processes. **Desktop Publishing (DTP)** software such as Adobe PageMaker® and QuarkXpress™ has permanently changed the graphics and print industries. Computers have given everyone who owns one the opportunity to try his or her hand at being a graphic designer. There is, of course, a great difference between a skilled professional and a dabbler—the product is usually a dead give-away!

Graphics for fashion does not always require reproduction. The internal graphics presentations don't always have to be reproduced, but the external ones do. Therefore, the amount of information that a fashion designer has to have at hand varies with the intent of the presentation. Obviously, developing presentation materials for reproduction requires special consideration and information. Many books on graphic design for production are available and the printing company itself can be very helpful in offering guidelines for reproduction based on their own equipment. The suggestions offered here, in a text for fashion designers, are only a first step toward creating well-designed graphic presentations.

When a designer begins to develop an idea, he or she already knows what has to be communicated—the type of product that is required. He or she will also know exactly who the audience for the presentation is going to be. Next, the designer has to think about the materials that he or she has on hand or those that need to be collected. Designers are great collectors of visual information. They keep file folders of magazine swipes, sketches, swatches, postcards, greeting cards, and assorted items of interest. While working on a new line, they often use images from their files to build visual ideas on a bulletin board. The bulletin board grows as the designer clarifies the direction for the upcoming season. When the time comes to generate a formal presentation board, many of the materials are already at hand.

The images that a designer selects and/or creates are based on the communication goals of each type of board. The basic materials that need to be gathered for a presentation are:

Images for mood and inspiration
Color indicators (yarns, paint chips, etc.)
Textile swatches or renderings
Flat renderings of silhouettes
Ground color and texture
Type style

Organization and Composition

The materials for the presentation board are organized according to a plan or composition. Traditionally, designers have used a collage method of assembling boards. They gather the images, yarns, swatches or textile renderings, flats, and illustrations and cut and paste them onto illustration board, corrugated board, or foam core. The board is covered in a ground material, paper or fabric. The selected ground cover has to work with the overall image or mood of the board. For example, if you are creating a color storyboard and the focus is on pastel colors, the ground cover should be chosen in keeping with the pastel mood; obviously, black or a bright primary color will diminish the effect.

Some of the components for the board may be hand drawn, some are swipes from magazines or travel brochures, and some are computer-generated images or images that have been scanned into the computer and manipulated. Sometimes the components are placed onto a separate piece of foam core that has been covered with a ground material and placed on the ground board for a more three-dimensional effect.

Lettering can be calligraphy—a press-on variety or a computer printout that is cut out and pasted on. The **font** that is selected for use in the presentation should also relate to the style of the overall image (see Figure 8–4). Typography can dress up the words and greatly increase the overall impact of the finished work, so it should be chosen with care. If the group you are presenting is in a feminine, romantic mood, don't choose a Futura Bold typeface; perhaps a finer italic or script would work better. Display type is decorative or ornamental and is used primarily for headings and large-size copy. Look for interesting type styles in graphics and desktop publishing software programs or buy a separate package that includes unusual fonts. Be careful mixing

Quirky, Playful

Techno

BOLD, MASCULINE

Simple, Clean

Romantic

Figure 8–4   The type of font chosen for a presentation helps to create a feeling about the product.

typefaces. All parts of the presentation should be coherent and relate to the general mood of the product you are trying to sell.

Consider the size of the final presentation board as soon as you start thinking about composition and content. Try to use standard board sizes that are available in art supply stores. If your presentation is computer generated rather than collage, the primary concern will be the paper size accepted by the printer. Standard size is $8\frac{1}{2} \times 11$, but many printers also use 11×17 paper. Decide if your presentation will be made up of a number of individual sheets that are mounted separately, or if the sheets will be tiled, or laid one next to another with the final image running fluidly over the separate pages. If the presentation board is to include a fabric story as well as a line board and a merchandising board, you may consider three individual compositions that make up a related triptych (see Plate 28).

Any graphics format, whether collage or completely computer generated, requires an aesthetically pleasing composition. A thumbnail sketch is usually the first step in organizing ideas and components. A grid can be developed to show the exact size and placement of each of the images. The images can be **scaled** up and down in size to fit the grid. They can also be **cropped** to fit the grid so don't be too concerned if the original images aren't the proper sizes for the grid you are developing. A good color copier is a great help at this stage of production because you can scale up and down, increasing or decreasing the size of the image as you copy. Remember to indicate text size and placement on your mock-up.

Sometimes a designer is given a specific style or format to work within based on company policy. This takes some of the guesswork out of the process, but offers its own limitations.

Great care should be taken to control the focal point and the way the eye of the viewer will travel around the board. **White space**, or places in the presentation where the eye can rest, are very important and contribute to a positive result. On the other hand, if the eye rests too much, the information presented on the board loses importance. The goal is to captivate and capture the viewer; to keep his or her eye moving within the confines of the board for as long as possible.

COMPUTER-GENERATED PRESENTATIONS

Some designers are presently creating presentations that are entirely computer generated (see Figure 8–5). This means that the collage is created right on the screen rather than by traditional

Figure 8–5   "Vision" Apparel CAD system is one of the many programs that can be used to prepare a presentation (Courtesy of Info Design Inc.)

cut-and-paste methods. Fabric boards and line boards are particularly suited to CAD development because the textiles and silhouettes are often created and rendered using CAD systems. As CAD becomes more and more universal, computer-generated professional presentation boards will become the norm (see Plate 29).

Presentation Boards

Certain advantages to using a computer to assemble a presentation board are listed below.

1. Software packages such as Adobe Photoshop™ have enormous potential to manipulate images. The tools have the ability to add many special effects to the presentation as a whole as well as to the individual components of the presentation.
2. A grid can be easily created in a graphics program so the mock-up is not difficult to generate. Changes and new versions are quick and easy to come up with.
3. The cropping and resizing functions are a great asset in helping with the relationships among the component images.
4. Type is easy to establish, alter, and replace with very little investment of time and expense. Be careful to generate the type in a vector-based or DTP program so that the type is not **pixelated** when printed out.

Of course, certain challenges have to be addressed when working with a computer-generated presentation board. The relationships among the resolution of the scanner, the screen, and the printer are often a mystery to the novice designer. In addition, the size of the scanned image as it relates to screen size and the size of the printed image are also issues that have to be played with. Finally, there is the problem of matching color from swatch to screen to printout.

A few helpful hints follow, but a great deal is learned through trial, error, and success. When color scanning, use the smallest area of the image possible and scan at the lowest comfortable resolution. A scanned image takes up a great amount of memory; the higher the resolution and size of that image, the more memory is required. A black-and-white or greyscale scan should not pose too much of a problem with memory.

The relationship between the size of the scanned image, the resolution, and the screen size of the image can be understood by the following example: If the original size of the image is 5 inches wide and you scan it in at 72 dpi, then it will take up 5×72 or 360 pixels horizontally or vertically on the screen. Since your screen resolution is also 72, the size of the image will be 5 inches. If you are scanning the same 5-inch image at a resolution of 144 dpi, it will take up 5×144 or 720 pixels horizontally or vertically on the screen. 720 ÷ 72 = 10, so the image will be 10 inches long or wide on the screen.

These can be daunting issues, but a little practice will help in the early stages. Since the screen resolution is 72 dots per inch, if you print at 72 dpi, you'll maintain a one-to-one ratio and maintain screen size. This can sometimes be a problem because you are printing at a low resolution so the printout may be pixelated; that is, the edges appear to be jagged and choppy and the detail is of low quality. One way of working around this is to work on screen at twice the intended size and then print at half scale. When you are working on the mock-up, print it out in black and white even before you place the images to check for scale.

As for color, if you don't have sophisticated color-calibration software, spend some time creating a printer palette. Work with software that supports the PANTONE TEXTILE Color System® or another numerically based color system (such as HSV, RGB or CMYK). Create a screen palette by working with different colors on the screen until they match your physical swatches, paint chips, or seasonal color card. Save the document as "Screen Color."

Next, start a new document and paint at least a hundred color swatches on the page; a wide brush stroke of color will do. Select colors that are close variations of each other, simulating the colors in your seasonal palette or swatches. Save the document as "Print Color" and print it out. Compare the printout with your color swatches. You should be able to find some matches in your printout. If not, add more colors to the document until you are satisfied. Since all of the colors in your Print Color document will have HSV, RGB, PANTONE Color System, or CMYK numbers associated with them, you can make the color substitutions on screen right before you print your final design work.

With this method, the Screen Color document will have the correct colors on screen, but will print incorrectly. The Print Color document will have the incorrect colors on the screen, but will print correctly. This process can be painstaking, but if you work with a seasonal palette and use the same colors again and again, it only has to be undertaken once each season.

CAD designers have had to adapt to this process and can usually work with the incorrect color on the screen knowing that once it is printed out the color will be accurate. Printing conditions change and color output also changes so this is not a foolproof method, but evolving technology is on the way to solving many color printing problems. Off-the-shelf software is available that prints a complete range of colors surrounding one particular shade to help with monitor-to-printer color-matching problems.

Photo credit: Laura Satori

Interview with
Kenji Takabayashi
Eastern Regional Support Manager,
Computer Design, Inc.

Takabayashi: I've been with Computer Design for eight years. Every CAD company has its hot shot demonstrators. I guess that's really what I am, although I wear a couple of other hats. We sell (CAD systems) to many companies so I've gotten to meet a lot of famous designers and work with a lot of talented people in different facets of the industry. Even Mattel uses the system for Barbie clothes which is kind of neat.

R.W.C.:   Did you have to have a fashion background in order to be able to do these demonstrations?

Takabayashi: When I first started, I had no fashion sense, and I would do a plaid and make it really bright acid green with red, and the salespeople would just squirm and the designers would sit there in disbelief. Now, I cater my demonstration or project toward the company. The more I know about the company I'm doing the demo for, the better the impression I can leave. If I'm doing a demo for a better men's sportswear company, I'm not going to show them a duck print that I did for a children's wear company. I'm going to do very fine wovens and different colorways and maybe some tie design and stuff like that. In the beginning, I didn't know what to show. I've just gained experience working with different clients.

R.W.C.:   Do you work solely for CDI or do you also do freelance work as well?

Takabayashi: I do freelance projects in my off hours for various companies. I do textile recolorings and quite a lot of texture mapping. It's really taken off in the home furnishing industry. Most of the apparel work is usually very tight, finished artwork like textile designs and merchandising boards. I've done some fashion illustration for some companies, too.

R.W.C.: When you create a presentation board, is it done through using cut-and-paste methods or do you assemble the whole thing on the system and print one sheet from the computer image?

Takabayashi: I like to use the computer. I would say that a majority of companies, regardless of whose system they use, print their stuff out and cut it out and still do it the old way. I don't like that method. I think that when you do it the old way—print the stuff out, cut it out, and put it on the board—it looks nice, but there are special effects and graphics that you can include in the image when it's all done on the computer. But when you do assemble something as a total file, you generally start to develop a very large file. When I assemble something that's 24 inches by 24 inches for the Iris (printer), that file at 300 dpi is going to be about 100 megabytes. That can be a problem for some systems.

R.W.C.: What is the job market like now for people coming out of school and looking for jobs?

Takabayashi: There are tons of jobs available. People are getting placed immediately. At any given time for the last six months, there's been quite a few openings at various companies.

R.W.C.: Do you find that most apparel companies are using CAD these days?

Takabayashi: Some of the collection designers still are adverse to the technology a little bit. Alexander Julian was one of the more open designers toward this technology; he actually works with it in some cases. He's very pro CAD; he actually has his system set up in his country house in Connecticut. These systems are starting to be able to render so much more detail; the presentations are beautiful. People are starting to buckle to the fact that they can't say it's not good enough anymore. There's really no argument.

R.W.C.: How do you approach a CAD job? Do you break it down into a series of operations?

Takabayashi: I will look at the project and break it down into steps before I scan it in. It's rare that I get surprised by an image that I scan, I kind of know what's going to happen. There are some things that the CAD system can't do, like a very complex watercolor print. Well, you can do it on a CAD system but it might take you three or four days. To paint it will take a day. So you have to separate the really difficult work from the work that you can do in a half hour. It's really a time management issue to figure out which best utilizes the CAD operator and system.

R.W.C.: How often do you just start from scratch and not use the scanner or artwork, but build the artwork, just using the system?

Takabayashi: Quite a lot. There are so many different effects that you can add nowadays. You can create magnificent tie-dye and watercolor effects and very tight paisley designs. In some cases, you can work so finely that only the best printing mills are able to print it. So that's another thing that people have to be careful of. The person that is working the CAD system has to know what the production house or what the engraving mill can produce.

R.W.C.:   What about CAD for representational purposes and visualization of virtual products? Do you see catalogues developed without samples? Is this really a way that apparel manufacturers can increase profits?

Takabayashi: What these systems are doing is allowing them to get the product out quicker, and in some cases, allowing them to help manufacture the product and streamline everything. Where they had to do it by traditional methods, the cycle would take many weeks to up to two months to get a strike-off back. If it was wrong, they had to wait another cycle. With these systems, along with high-speed communications, you can get approval within a few weeks. The cycle is cut way down. So that's a plus. Express and Claiborne are both very technologically driven companies, and excellent clients of ours. They are looking at cutting that pipeline to a very short period of time, where they are using the system to do the textile design and send that textile design directly to the Orient via a high-speed communication device. They'll send a file to Hong Kong in minutes. That's the direction for the future.

R.W.C.:   What about the trend toward digital printing, will there be an end to engraving, and screens?

Takabayashi: I think so. I absolutely think so. I think it's really close today, but there will be a time when systems will print, on demand, small lots for sampling as well as huge production. When digital printing takes over there will be a change in the way people work. The products will not have the production limitations that they do now. You'll be able to do a photograph on a dress for the same price as a six-color screen. You won't have all the plates and all the costs of burning and engraving the cylinders. It's definitely the way it's going.

R.W.C.:   What are manufacturers looking for in the CAD systems they buy?

Takabayashi: There are so many CAD systems out there now—there are about 25 to 30 different ones. And each one has a niche. There are Macintoshes for people that like Macs, there are PCs, there are workstations like ours. But somewhere down the line, apparel manufacturers are going to want to go all the way from design to production to catalogue on one system. They'll want the system to be easy to use and to do everything and more. There are a lot of people that say, "I've only got $25,000, so I'm going to buy this . . . " And then six months down the road, "Well you know, that catalogue cost me $75,000 to produce. Why couldn't I do that on my machine? Well, we don't have enough resolution to do that . . . " So the manufacturer always has to think long term.

R.W.C.:   How did you get your start as a CAD artist?

Takabayashi: My background is fantasy illustration. I used to be a graffiti artist. I don't use a pen, I use a mouse all the time. It's an optical mouse—laser driven. I think I like the mouse because the spray can was about the same width. Then I studied illustration at the High School for Art and Design. After that, I worked as an intern at Time Life. And I worked for Chris Meer, who was the publisher of People magazine. Truth be told, I really would rather be working for

Spielberg. I actually have a picture in my office of Spielberg that I doctored up with my CAD system.

Computer-Generated Catalogues

When buyers source the market for merchandise, they look at thousands of garments in their buying categories (see Chapter 4) during their search. There are certain companies that they go back to season after season and others that they test out for product performance in their stores. Manufacturers compete against one another for the buyers' open-to-buy. If buyers can leave a company's showroom or exhibit area with images on paper of the products that they just saw, they will have a way to remember a particular company's designs when they are ready to write their orders.

Manufacturers have found that developing an in-house product catalogue has been well worth the time and effort. Cost, however, has been a great inhibitor. A photo shoot would have to be set up and an image taken of each item in the product line. The images would then have to be composed, type would be added, and the printing company would make the color separations and print the catalogue. The product samples would all have to be completed far in advance of the season to allow for catalogue development time. Production costs for this type of process are very high.

Designers who use CAD to develop fabrics and technical drawings are able to import these images into desktop publishing programs in order to develop their own camera-ready artwork for printing (see Figure 8–6). Some companies combine old and new processes; they generate the images of the clothing on their CAD stations and then let the printer's graphics department work with layout and type. Other companies scan photographs into their systems and then use texture mapping to replace old garments with new and then these "virtual images" go to the printer. This trend in developing a virtual product, or one that does not really exist in sample form, promises to save the apparel industry a great deal of money by bypassing many of the traditional product development processes.

Some CAD suppliers have developed specific programs that designers can use to develop catalogues. Since the images of the fabrics, the spec drawings, and the illustrations are all stored in the CAD system, all documents relating to a certain style are accessible (see Chapter 3). Developing a catalogue page, then, becomes a relatively simple matter of setting up the style of the page and bringing the various components into it. Figure 8–7 shows a CAD system that has a catalogue development component.

Direct merchants such as Tweeds, J. Crew, and many others use their catalogues to sell their products externally, or directly to the public. These companies often have in-house art and graphics departments that work with desktop publishing software to devel-

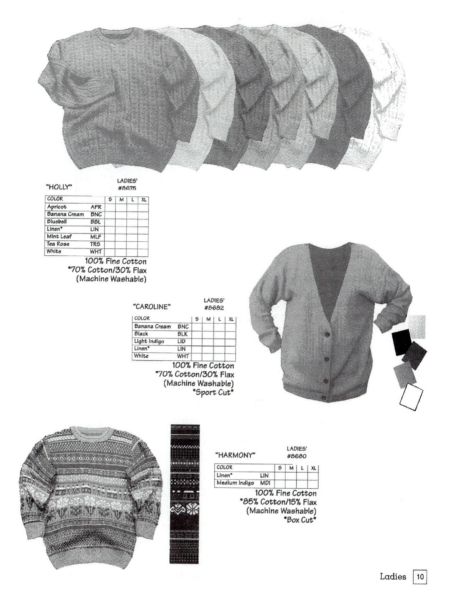

Figure 8–6 Cad-generated catalogue page using scanned photographs and texture mapping. Images were imported into a DTP program before final printing (Courtesy of Alps Sportswear Mfg. Co., Inc.)

op their catalogues. Lands' End is a direct merchant that has taken a bold step in showing a CAD-generated virtual product on the cover of one of its catalogues (see Plate 30). This use of CAD technology in catalogue development promises to become more and more widespread as companies begin to realize its advantages.

Multimedia and 3-D Presentations

As technology evolves, many companies are using the new developments as a way of merchandising and marketing their products. Fashion shows can be developed from digital images and

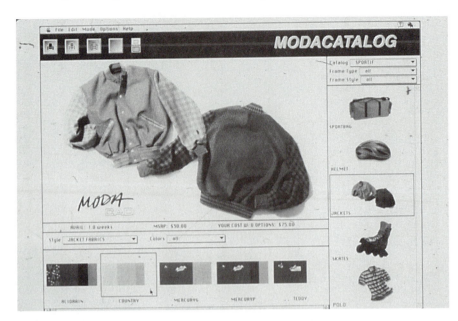

Figure 8–7 Catalogue development software, Moda CATALOG, includes live-action multimedia components that are interactive (Courtesy of ModaCAD™)

virtual garments created on the bodies of videotapes or photographs of super models. Virtual fashion shows developed from digital images and videotapes of supermodels dressed in virtual garments. Scores of special effects including sound can be added using personal computers. Store interiors can be photographed using a digital camera and a person can shop the contents of a store zooming in on a particular product that is hanging on a rack or stacked on a display unit. This product can be rotated three-dimensionally to be seen from all sides.

Although the use of this technology is not yet widespread in the apparel industry, there seems to be no doubt about its potential. One of the most exciting aspects of working in today's garment industry is being involved with the absorption of all of the world's newest technologies into the fashion field. We look forward to the next step.

STUDY QUESTIONS AND PROBLEMS

1. Create an 8½ by 11 style sheet using one of the flat drawings from the previous chapter and combining it with a fabric swatch created in Chapter 6. Show two colorways and add type.

2. Design a logo for a children's line and generate a label and a hang tag.

3. Plan a presentation using one of the silhouette groups from Chapter 7 and the textiles designed in Chapter 6. Select and organize the components and create a mock-up of each page on the computer. Try organizing your presentation using two to four separate pages that relate to each other. Print out and mount your final results on foam core.

Glossary

Additive color   The colors produced by light—RGB (red, green, blue)—that when mixed together create white.

Agile manufacturing   Garment production based on cutting and manufacturing small lots and resulting in quick turnover of merchandise; flexible manufacturing.

Bar coding   A series of vertical bars that identify a merchandise category, the name of the manufacturer, and the item.

Bit depth   The amount of memory the computer allocates to each pixel.

Bitmapped image   An image created in a raster-based program by filling pixels.

Blanket   In textile production, a sample of a weave structure produced for approval.

Block   A basic pattern shape that can be manipulated to create patterns for most garments; sloper.

Bottom-weight fabrics   Textiles that are used to produce skirts, pants, jackets, and other "bottoms."

Branded merchandise   In retail, a product that has a trade name, label, or symbol as opposed to private label merchandise.

CAD   Computer-aided design.

Calibration   Setting color on computer screens and/or color printers so that they match each other.

CAM   Computer-aided manufacturing.

Chroma   Intensity of color, concentration of hue; also known as saturation.

CIELAB   A uniform color space that allows for the measurement and numeric coding of color.

CIM   Computer-integrated manufacturing that implies information sharing through computer networks through all levels of design and production.

Cloth spreader   Machinery that lays out and stacks fabric for cutting.

Colorimeter   An instrument that measures color.

Color reduction   Decreasing the number of colors in an image.

Colorway   Color variation of a design.

Companion print   Textile print designs that are meant to coordinate with each other.

Concept board   A presentation that communicates the mood or feeling of a potential product line; mood board; storyboard.

Connectivity   Information sharing among all phases of design and manufacture.

Coordinated print   Print designs that are meant to be used together; related in color and subject matter.

Crop   Trimming down undesirable parts of an image.

Croquis   In textile design, the original painting done by the artist; in fashion design, the original, unfinished sketch.

Cut and sew   In knitting, fabric produced as yard goods which is then cut into pattern shapes and sewn together.

Cut path   A plan for accurate and efficient cloth cutting by machine.

Cyan, magenta, yellow, and black (CMYK) The process colors used by the printing industry. See Subtractive color.

Database marketing   Reaching customers by way of a computerized information system that tracks individual buying habits and selections.

Demographics   The study of the vital statistics of a population.

Densitometer   A photoelectric instrument that measures the amount of light absorbed by a color or by an image.

Desktop publishing (DTP)   Computer-generated design and layout of material for printing and/or publishing.

Digital interactive television   Television cable connected to telephone lines for interactive communication.

Digitizing   Entering information about the shape of a pattern part into a computer based on points around the edges and along interior lines.

Electronic data interchange (EDI)   Information shared among computers.

Electronic body scanning   The use of video input to define an individual's body shape to a computer.

Electronic shopping   Purchasing product by way of a computer, telephone wires, modem, and/or television.

Electronic sourcing   On-line information on market resources.

Ends   The vertical yarns in fabric that run parallel to the finished edge or selvage; also called warp.

Fabric simulation   A computer-generated rendering of a textile design and/or weave.

Flat line rendering   A flat, technical sketch of a garment that shows construction detail.

Flexible manufacturing   Garment production based on cutting and manufacturing small lots and resulting in quick turnover of merchandise; agile manufacturing.

Font   Type style used in graphic design.

Full fashioned   In knitting, garment parts that are knitted to shape and then seamed together.

Garment-moving technology   A conveyer system in a manufacturing plant that moves garment parts from operator to operator for construction.

Gauge   In knitted fabrics, the closeness of the needles used by a knitting machine; the fineness of the cloth.

Geographics   The statistical study of the habitat location of a population.

Grade rules   In pattern grading, the amount of increase or decrease in dimension at designated points along the exterior and interior of a pattern part for purposes of sizing.

Griege goods   Unprocessed fabric that has not been finished, bleached, or treated.

Half drop   A layout for print design in which the original motif is repeated halfway down the side of the vertical measurement of the overall motif.

Hand loom   In textile production, a sample of a weave produced for approval; blanket.

Hue   The name of a color.

Hue, Value, Chroma (HVC)   A numeric method of coding color created by light as in a television or computer screen.

Illustration system   A CAD system that uses a large drawing pad and stylus to allow a designer to simulate drawing by hand; sketchpad system.

Industry-specific   A CAD system used only in apparel; not available to the public. See Proprietary.

Interconnectivity   Ability of computer systems to share information.

Knit down   In knitting, the sample produced for approval.

Lab dip   Testing done by a dye house for color accuracy that is sent back to the design room for approval.

Laser cutter   A cutting machine that uses laser beams to cut cloth.

Lay plan   A plan for laying down fabric and all the pattern parts to cut the required number of garments.

Light box   An environment that provides stable lighting conditions for color viewing and matching.

Marker   An arrangement of all the pattern parts required to cut garment(s).

Markermaking system   A computerized arrangement of pattern pieces for maximum fabric utilization.

Marketplace   The location for buying and selling goods and/or merchandise.

Market positioning   The selection of a clothing category, price point, and point of sale for a product line.

Merchandise information systems (MIS)   Electronic networking of manufacturing data.

Mill end   A two- to three-yard textile sample that a designer receives from a mill.

Mood board   A presentation that communicates the mood or feeling of a potential product line; concept board.

Motif A design unit or design element.

Nested pattern Patterns that have been graded and stacked inside one another.

Novelty fabrics Nonstaple fabrics such as prints, special weaves, and unusual textures and blends.

Off-the-shelf Software that is commerically available to the pulbic.

Pattern design system (PDS) A CAD system used to draft and manipulate patterns.

Pattern generation system (PGS) A CAD system that creates or manipulates patterns based on the input of verbal and numerical directions.

Pattern grading Scaling a sample size pattern up or down to create all the necessary sizes.

Peg plan A stitch-by-stitch indication of the threading pattern for weaving cloth.

Picks The horizontal yarns that run from selvage to selvage in weaving; also called filling or weft.

Pitching Method of establishing colorways based on movement around the color wheel.

Pixelated An image that has poorly defined, jagged edges produced in a raster-based paint program.

Plotter An output device that draws pattern parts on paper after they have been worked with in a CAD system.

Pre-production processes and systems Used to create and store technical information required for production of textiles or garments.

Primary market Producers of the raw materials used in manufacturing clothing.

Private label Merchandise that has been produced by a retailer under its own label.

Process colors Colors used by the printing industry; CMYK (cyan, magenta, yellow, and black). See Subtractive color.

Product data management (PDM) Integrated computer systems that allow information to be shared by all phases of design and manufacture.

Proprietary CAD system Software and hardware that has been developed by a private supplier to industry. See Industry-specific.

Psychographics The statistical study of a population's attitudes and values.

Quarter drop A layout for print design in which the original motif is repeated one fourth of the way down the side of the vertical measurement of the overall motif.

Quick response technology (QRT) Systems based on computer networking that help to shorten the ordering and manufacturing cycle.

Radio frequency tagging Identification embedded in garment parts that can only be read by computers.

Raster-based image Computer-generated line and shape that is defined by individual pixels that have each been colored in.

Red, green, blue (RGB) The primary hues used by a computer to create color with light. See Additive color.

Repeat In textile print design, the duplication and placement of a motif or design so that it can continuously cover the surface of the fabric when it is printed.

Retail market Selling of finished product to the consumer.

Robotics The use of mechanical devices for garment production that is usually handled by humans.

Saturation Intensity of color, concentration of hue; also known as chroma.

Scale Increasing or decreasing the overall size of an image.

Secondary market Producers of finished apparel.

Silhouette The overall shape of a design as it appears on the body.

Sketchpad system See Illustration system.

Sloper A basic pattern shape that can be manipulated to create patterns for most garments; block.

Sourcing (the market) The act of seeking out and purchasing the materials and services necessary for the production, marketing, and merchandising of a product.

Specifications sheet (spec sheet) A document containing technical information about a garment.

Spectrophotometer An instrument that measures light at points on the visual spectrum.

Staples Goods that are used by a company on a continual basis. Staples can be raw materials, textiles, or finished products.

Stockeeping unit (SKU) Used in retail to track inventory and to assess the number of pieces a store owns or will own.

Strike-off In textile printing, a sample of the fabric produced for design and color approval.

Subtractive color The process by which we see color created by pigment; the net color that is reflected back to the eye is the result of all other colors being absorbed (subtracted) by the pigment.

Sweater graph In knitting, a grid that shows the color and placement of each stitch.

Swipe An image torn from a magazine, brochure, or other printed material used to show the mood or direction of a design idea.

Tagged image file format (TIFF) The computer file format accepted for general use by the textile printing industry.

Target customers The individuals that a company directs its marketing strategies toward; the most desired consumers of a company's product.

Textile design system A CAD system used to design woven and/or knitted fabrics including prints.

Texture mapping The process by which a computer replaces the fabric of a garment in a photograph with a new textile design while maintaining the folds and shading of the original image.

Theme board A presentation that offers a topical direction for development of a design idea.

Top-weight fabrics Textiles that are used to produce blouses, tops, shirts.

Turnkey system A CAD system in which the software and the hardware is proprietary.

Value The shade of a color; lightness or brightness.

Vector-based image Line or objects created by a computer through the definition of mathematical formulas describing those lines and/or objects.

Virtual imaging Creating or manipulating the image of a product using a computer.

Virtual product A garment created by computer for which a sample has not been made.

Warp The vertical yarns in fabric that run parallel to the finished edge or selvage.

Weave diagram A thread-by-thread diagram of the structure of a woven textile design.

Weft The horizontal yarns that run from selvage to selvage in weaving; also called filling.

Weighing-in In creating colorways for print design, the process of maintaining value and chroma that is similar to the original; only the hues change.

White space The area in a graphic design that the image does not occupy.

BIBLIOGRAPHY

ALDRICH, WINIFRED, ed., *CAD in Clothing and Textiles*. Oxford, England: BSP Professional Books, 1992.

CHIJIIWA, HIDEAKI, *Color Harmony, A Guide to Creative Color Combinations*. Rockport, MA: Rockport Publishers, 1992.

FISHER, RICHARD, and DOROTHY WOLFTHAL, *Textile Print Design*. New York: Fairchild Publications, 1987.

FRINGS, GINI STEPHENS, *Fashion from Concept to Consumer* (4th ed.) Englewood Cliffs, NJ: Prentice Hall, 1994.

GRAY, STEPHEN, *The Benefits of Computer-Aided Design and Manufacture.* London: The Design Council, 1992.

HAFER, GARY R., "The Effect of Computer Aided Design Systems on the Visual Design Processes and Visual Communication in Apparel Manufacturing Companies." Thesis. University of North Carolina, 1992.

JARNOW, JEANETTE, and MIRIAM GUERREIRO, *Inside the Fashion Business* (5th ed.). New York: Macmillan, 1991.

JERNIGAN, MARIAN H., and CYNTHIA R. EASTERLING, *Fashion Merchandising and Marketing.* New York: Macmillan, 1990.

JOSEPH, MARJORIE L., *Essentials of Textiles* (4th ed.). New York: Holt, Rinehart and Winston, 1988.

JOYCE, CAROL, *Textile Design: The Complete Guide to Printed Textiles for Apparel and Home Furnishings.* New York: Watson-Guptill Publications, 1993.

KOTLER, PHILIP, GARY ARMSTRONG, and RICHARD G. STARR, JR., *Principles of Marketing* (5th ed.). Englewood Cliffs, NJ: Prentice Hall, 1991.

PHILLIPS, PETER, and GILLIAN BUNCE, *Repeat Patterns, A Manual for Designers, Artists and Architects.* London: Thames and Hudson, Ltd., 1993.

PICKEN, MARY BROOKS, *The Fashion Dictionary.* New York: Funk and Wagnalls, 1973.

PIPES, ALAN, *Production for Graphic Designers.* Englewood Cliffs, NJ: Prentice Hall, 1993.

SMITH, ROBERT CHARLES, *Basic Graphic Design* (2nd ed.). Englewood Cliffs, NJ: Prentice Hall, 1993.

TATE, SHARON LEE, *Inside Fashion Design* (3rd ed.). New York: Harper and Row Publishers, 1989.

WINTERS, ARTHUR A., and STANLEY GOODMAN, *Fashion Advertising and Promotion* (6th ed.). New York: Fairchild Publications, 1984.

FOOTNOTES

1. National Knitwear Association and A. Grudier Consulting, "Survey Reports CAD Use Up," *FabriCAD Update*, vol. 3, no. 4 (July 1995), p. 3.
2. Allison Grudier, "Making Sense of the CAD Marketplace," *Bobbin Magazine* (July 1994), p. 68.
3. National Knitwear Association and A. Grudier Consulting, "Survey Reports CAD Use Up," p. 3.
4. Michele Kozey and Stephen Sprinkle, "Competitive Computing, CAD Creates Flexible Quick Response," *Apparel Industry Magazine* (April 1993), p. 26.
5. John Wiater, "Tomorrow Is Here," *Bobbin Magazine* (July 1995), p. 37.
6. Interview, Walter Wilhelm, Gerber Garment Technology, March 23, 1995.

7. Ibid.

8. "*Bobbin Magazine's* 1995 Apparel and Textile Industry-Specific Computer Software Survey," *Bobbin Magazine* (July 1995), p. 36A.

9. John W. DeWitt, "Freeing the Bottleneck," *Apparel Industry Magazine*, vol. 56 (March 1995), p. 3.

10. Linda Friedman, "Cad/Cam Technology Paints a New Picture," *Bobbin Magazine* (April 1991), p. 88.

11. John Wiater, "Tomorrow Is Here," p. 38.

12. Georgia Lee, "Bobbin Show Stresses High Tech," *Women's Wear Daily*, vol. 168, no. 65 (October 3, 1994), p. 20.

13. John W. DeWitt, "(TC)^2 Will Demo Agility Through Partnerships," *Apparel Industry Magazine* (August 1994), p. 87.

14. "World Retailing: Serious Seventeen Remain So," *Chain Store Executive* (January 1995), p. 4.

15. Lenda Jo Anderson and Mike Yodaro, "Sourcing in the Year 2000," *Bobbin Magazine* (May 1995), pp. 74–80.

16. Ibid.

17. Jules Abend, "Private Labels, Brands Square Off," *Bobbin Magazine* (June 1995), p. 66.

18. Susan Reda, "Interactive Shopping: Will Consumers Catch Up with the Technology," *In Stores*, vol. 77, no. 3 (March 1995), pp. 20–24.

19. Ibid.

20. "Non-Store Retailing: Catch the New Wave," *Chain Store Age Executive*, vol. 70, no. 8 (Section 2) (August 1994), pp. 16A-18A.

21. Josef Albers. *Interaction of Color.* Yale University Press, 1975.

22. Mary Brooks Picken. *The Fashion Dictionary.* New York: Funk and Wagnalls, 1973. p. 329.

Index